T0148254

I'm not fat, I'm just
big boned and other lies
we tell ourselves

I'm not fat, I'm just big boned and other lies we tell ourselves

Overcoming a lifelong battle with obesity

Leticia Remauro

iUniverse, Inc.
Bloomington

I'm not fat, I'm just big boned and other lies we tell ourselves
Overcoming a lifelong battle with obesity

iUniverse books may be ordered through booksellers or by contacting:

iUniverse
1663 Liberty Drive
Bloomington, IN 47403
www.iuniverse.com
1-800-Authors (1-800-288-4677)

ISBN: 978-1-4620-1552-8 (pbk)
ISBN: 978-1-4620-1553-5 (ebk)

Printed in the United States of America

iUniverse rev. date: 06/02/2011

This book is dedicated to my daughter Jennifer.
I gave her life and she returned the favor
by giving my life back to me.

Also by Leticia Remauro:
Patric's Saga—The Story of Brian Boru
and His Mystical Wife, Kormlada

PREFACE

When I first decided to write this book it was because I wanted to share my weight loss experience with others. I figured that if I could overcome a life long struggle with obesity then others could as well. I compiled all my tips in one place hoping that after people read them they would understand that weight loss is an achievable goal. The odd thing is, the more I wrote the more I realized that it wasn't a diet program alone that helped me to lose weight—it was the fact that I had finally stopped lying to myself about why I was fat in the first place.

It wasn't easy for me to admit that I was abusing myself or to recognize the reasons that I did. That acknowledgement has changed my relationship with food and the people in my life. I finally realized that if I wanted to get healthy I needed to stop lying to myself.

What you will read on these pages is my story. The story of who I was and what it took to make me who I am today. Some of the stories are funny; others less so, but all are true. They are my stories and I hope that when you read them you will find something to inspire you toward a healthier lifestyle.

Whether you have ten or one hundred ten pounds to lose, the tips in this book can help you. However, this is not a diet book. It won't give you the list of items you need to eat to lose weight. It doesn't promise a pain free way to fit into those great jeans or killer black dress. What it will do is help you understand that you deserve to enjoy your life. There is no reason to beat yourself up over past failures or even the fact that you need to lose weight now. It will show you that no matter how big your past mistakes seem, they can be overcome as long as you believe in yourself.

I would like to say I had fun writing this book, but I can't. It was difficult for me to put myself out there for others to judge—especially since I am a quasi-public figure in my community. What I will say is that I am happy that I wrote this book. It helped me to face things that most people prefer to keep hidden. We all have little lies that we tell ourselves to make us feel better. Now mine are out in the open. I hope that by reading about them you will be willing to face your own.

CHAPTER ONE

Building a Foundation for Obesity

"Clean your plate! There are children starving in China."

I don't remember the first time I heard that statement or who uttered it to me. All I can tell you is that it is indelibly etched into my psyche.

Most likely it was one of my grandmothers who first said it to me. Both were less than five feet tall and both tipped the scales at more than two hundred pounds.

My father's mother, Grandma Albert (I called both my grandmothers by their husband's name—don't ask me why), was from Naples. She liked to feed me Nutella (the hazelnut and chocolate spread that contains about two hundred calories per tablespoon) straight from the jar. She was an excellent cook, known best for her rabbit cacciatore. She grew the tomatoes and raised the rabbits, right in her backyard then cooked them up for Sunday dinner. Of the thousands of times she cooked for me, I don't think Grandma Albert ever served a bad meal. She was incapable of it.

My mother's mother, Grandma Blackie (Blackie was my grandfather's nickname—again, don't ask), was born in Boston. Her parents were from Sicily. She too was a cook, but she was best known for her baking. Her house always smelled of nutmeg and cinnamon. When she was younger she cooked in a restaurant. People would come from miles around for her potato and egg sandwiches or her fried veal cutlets. From the time I was born until she moved from her house in Cobble Hill, Brooklyn three decades later, there was always an abundance of food around the place just in case company dropped by.

Food is the center of the universe for Brooklyn, Italian families. Whether we are celebrating or grieving, we always have plenty of food for everyone. We cook it in our basement kitchens because the upstairs kitchen is for "show" (as is the formal living room and dining room furniture which are usually covered in plastic). We eat in courses of anti-pasto, pasta, meat, salad, fruit and dessert. And we eat in loud, boisterous packs of people all shouting over each other to be heard. It's no wonder the fondest memories of my childhood revolve around food. Unfortunately my relationship with food is also the source for much of the pain I have experienced in my life.

Both of my grandmothers had passive/aggressive personalities. In addition, both were contrary. They absolutely adored chubby babies, but if those chubby babies grew into obese kids there was hell to pay for both mother and child.

I was the first-born grandchild on both sides of the family. As such, the world revolved around me. Both grandmothers would fight for the chance to baby-sit me, and both would feed me until my little wrists were dimpled with fat and my little thighs had rolls in them.

I loved my grandmothers. They always had a sweet treat for me so long as I finished my meal. I grew up on such Italian delicacies as snails, calamari, tripe and cow's tongue. They would clap with glee when I ate every bit of the food from "the old country" they heaped on my plate. They proclaimed me their "Princepessa" (Little Princess) and I was happy that I made them proud.

My baby brother, Albert was a different story entirely. He was a "fussy eater" and a "problem child". The reason for those monikers—when he was full he simply refused to eat any more. He never had those rolls and creases as a baby. For that they blamed my mother.

My mother, Josephine (Josie for short) was a devastatingly beautiful woman. She had long, thick, black hair that shined in the light. Her eyes are shaped like almonds and she wore black eyeliner on her upper lids to accentuate their deep brown color. She had a killer figure, one that would put Sophia Loren's to shame and her smile (on the few occasions that I saw it), could melt anyone's heart. She was the great beauty of the family—unfortunately she never knew it.

I remember one time when my mother dropped us off at Grandma Blackie's house so she could sit for us. "Oh, don't you look nice," Grandma Blackie said to my mother as she took my brother's hand, circling his wrists loosely with her fingers as if she were testing him for the pot. "New hairdo?" My mother smiled then nodded proudly as she checked her reflection in the hallway mirror.

My mother's smile quickly faded when Grandma Blackie scooped my brother into her arms then walked him into the kitchen proclaiming, "Poor thing is light as a feather. No doubt he doesn't want to eat for the sitter you leave him with while you're at the beauty parlor getting your hair done."

The blow was delivered with stealth and precision worthy of a military sharp shooter. Grandma didn't bother to wait for a reaction. She knew she hit her target.

In my family words of praise are supposed to lull you into complacency so that when the information about what's really "wrong" with you is given, the deliverer doesn't feel like a bad guy. It's the perfect tactic to plant insecurity and doubt in a person who is self assured and successful.

Still dazed from the attack, my mother grabbed my arm then dragged me into the kitchen. I could feel her hand trembling as she bent down to try to smooth a wayward strand of hair back into my barrette. This grooming process took a particularly long time since I had kinky, curly hair that didn't always cooperate. She finally managed to get it under control with a bit of spit on her fingers. She kissed me then stood full up to face her attacker.

I wondered what she would say when her eyes met Grandma Blackie's. Grandma may have been shorter than Mommy, but she was a big, confident woman and she was holding my baby brother.

There was a long silence as Mommy weighed her options. She could say something that would start an argument which she could never win, or she could just leave and pretend nothing was said. I could feel the tension streaming from my mother's body. It seemed she was always tense around Grandma Blackie.

A few moments later my mother's shoulders sagged in defeat. She kissed my brother's head and whispered, "Be good for Grandma. Do everything she says."

My grandmother smiled smugly and Mommy turned on her heel then rubbed my head before exiting the kitchen. She stopped long enough to light a cigarette before marching down the hallway, mumbling to herself as she went. This time she didn't glance in the mirror when she passed it.

At that time I had no concept of passive/aggressive behavior or the things that go on between mothers and daughters. All I knew was that my grandmother was mad at my mother because my brother didn't like to eat. Well, if he was going to be uncooperative then it was up to me to make things better. I may have been young, but I knew my grandmother liked me, and if she liked me then I could use that to help my brother and mother out.

Albert and I sat at the white and gold formica top kitchen table where a Melmac bowl filled with lentils and pasta seemed to magically appear before us. I picked up my spoon and got ready to dig in but my brother grumbled that he wasn't hungry.

Grandma stood over us, her eyes narrowing as she unconsciously lifted her arm into the air so that the black strap of her bra could slip beneath her starched, flower-print house coat. Then she said, "Albert, you have to eat. You know, there are children in the world who don't have any food. Do you think they would complain if someone fed them?"

"It's good, Albert," I said after putting a big spoonful in my mouth. I smiled, hoping he would follow my lead.

My brother picked up his spoon and began moving the lentils around the bowl. Obviously he was too young to learn the lessons I already had. The first one was that children in the world would starve if you didn't eat everything on your plate, and the second was that the only way to get an ice cream cone with sprinkles in Grandma Blackie's house was to eat the food she gave you.

The adults in my family were interesting creatures. They fascinated me. They had a whole list of things they required you to be in order for them to be happy. The women were strong and beautiful. The men were strong too and they had a great appreciation for the beauty their women possessed. They always commented on it. In fact, the first word I learned in our native language was bella (beautiful). Beauty was very important. Almost equally important was intelligence. When you put them both together everything was perfect.

For the children of the family the list of demands included being "good" which could be confusing because being good could span from eating all your food to being able to recite a poem in front of twenty people at dinner. If you managed to recite it in Italian, you might even get some cash. You also needed to listen to the adults, keep yourself clean and not be shy in front of company.

I did my best to learn those lessons and to demonstrate my knowledge of them every chance I could. When I did it resulted in heaps of praise from all the adults in my world. I liked making them happy. I lived for nothing else. I was cute, I was smart and I was good. I could count to ten in Italian and say a few words at just the right time so that my grandparents could impress their "pisans" (friends from their home town). Best of all, I ate everything they put in front of me. All of this was "good" until I reached the ripe old age of eight-years-old. By then I was tipping the scales at around a hundred pounds. The cute, chubby baby was fast becoming an obese child and nobody seemed happy about that.

The first time I realized that my weight was an issue was when I was getting ready to receive my First Holy Communion. I was so chubby (that's code word for fat) that my mother had to purchase my dress from a high end retailer then pay a seamstress to let it out.

Apparently my father considered that to be a violation of the blue collar code. I remember the argument he had with my mother when he found out what she had done. Dad was a printer for the federal government. He didn't earn much money and every penny he brought home was earmarked for necessities. According to him, middle class Italians from

Brooklyn didn't shop in fancy department stores and they certainly didn't pay a seamstress to alter their clothes. Only rich, Manhattanites did that.

Mom had a different opinion about such things. She may not have known how to sew or cook, but she did have an incredible sense of style. She decorated our two bedroom walk-up on 58th Street, Brooklyn so perfectly that it could have been featured in Better Homes and Gardens.

Because she grew up in a house with eight other people where space was limited and money was tight, Mom insisted on creating dream bedrooms for my brother and me.

She did Albert's room in a racing motif with black and white checkered wallpaper and bright red furniture. Mine was done in princess pink. I even had a crown over my bed with pink chiffon ribbons hanging from it. My parents slept in the space that was supposed to be the dining room. Mom painted the walls bright tangerine and hung a pair of white louver doors from the ceiling to the floor to separate the room from the rest of the apartment. Unfortunately we could hear everything that was said behind those doors.

For as long as I can remember, I had a hard time sleeping by myself because I was afraid of the dark. I would stay up way past my bedtime listening to the sounds the house made. Sometimes I could hear my parents talking in their room. Usually they talked about how good I was in school, or how mature I was for my age. I liked listening to those conversations. It reassured me; made me feel loved. But the night my parents argued about me was a night I will never forget.

Dad was yelling at Mom, telling her that she couldn't continue to buy me expensive clothes because he couldn't afford to pay for them. Mom shot back by reminding Dad that she was paying for my dress with the money she earned drawing catalog ads from home for Montgomery Ward. She told him that the only stores that carried my size were the expensive department stores and that she wouldn't let me receive my First Holy Communion in a dress that didn't fit.

That didn't sit well with Dad. Like most Italian men, he had his pride and she had just wounded it because of me.

The argument went on for some time. Every word was like a blow to my grown-up induced, over inflated, ego. I lay in my bed crying until they finally went to sleep. When they did, I sneaked into the kitchen pantry, located the Chips A'hoy cookies then ate the entire bag. I hid the empty package at the bottom of the garbage pail so no one would see it.

CHAPTER TWO

My First Diet

Both of my parents were average size and my brother was skinny. Come to think of it, the only people in my family who were morbidly obese were me, both my grandmothers and Grandma Blackie's sister, Mary.

I'll never forget the day that Grandma Blackie and her sister finally decided I was too fat. I was just about nine-years-old. My aunt, Santa and my uncle Augie, had just returned from their honeymoon on some tropical island and they brought back a fresh coconut.

Coconuts aren't a staple in the Italian diet so everyone was quite excited by the gift. Everyone except the children that is. They preferred to play tag in the back yard rather than experience the worldly delight being fussed over in the dining room. I couldn't run around in the yard because I had Leg Perthes Disease—a disease that attacked the ball of the hip and turned it into mush. I had to wear a brace on my leg for a number of years so I rarely played with the other children. Instead I gathered around the table with the rest of the adults who were waiting for my father to remove the husk from the fruit (being an avid reader and an artist, my father always knew what to do with exotic things). Dad cracked the coconut with a hammer then poured the milk into a glass. Aunt Mary doled out the uneven pieces to the adults, but when I stepped up for my piece she refused.

"No, honey," she said, looking down at me like a judge handing down a prison sentence. "You won't like this. This is for the grownups. Why don't you go outside and play with the other kids?"

I couldn't believe it. Was it possible that someone was refusing to give me food? "But I want to taste it," I cried. "I'll like it. I won't waste it."

Aunt Mary picked up the plate containing the few remaining pieces of coconut. At first I thought she was going to give in to my pleading but then I realized my mistake. She handed the plate to my grandmother. "Angie," she said, "this stuff is very fattening. Do you want me to give her some?"

Grandma Blackie took the plate and walked into the kitchen. She exchanged a few words with Aunt Mary in Sicilian (an Italian dialect that escapes me to this day) then called back over her shoulder, "Tisha (my nickname), just go outside with the other kids and let the adults talk."

It became instantly clear to me that if I wanted a piece of coconut I would have to take a different tact. Being cute just wasn't enough and clearly my logical argument was falling on deaf ears. No, if I wanted coconut I would have to take my case to a higher authority and for that I needed to be sneaky.

I began to cry, which was the best way I knew to draw my mother's attention. You should know that aside from being devastatingly beautiful, my mother is one of the toughest people on the face of the earth. The woman could literally move a mountain to protect her children. No one, but no one, would dare do anything to spark her ire.

The tears had barely started to flow before my mother appeared at my side. "What's the matter?"

"Josie," Aunt Mary stammered, searching for the words to explain the situation without calling down my mother's wrath. "She wants a piece of coconut but she really is too heavy. This stuff is very fattening."

I could see the words sinking into my mother's brain. On too many occasions Mom was forced to defend me against both children and adults who had something to say about my weight. Not long before that day she had an argument with a neighbor lady who yelled at me for wetting her because I was sitting on the nozzle of an open fire hydrant while she was walking by.

"Look what you did, you little brat!" the woman spat as she dropped her grocery bags on the sidewalk so she could brush the water off her beautiful silk blouse. "Your mother should stop feeding you and teach you some manners! I should smack your fat face!"

I shrank back from the verbal assault and she stepped toward me. Suddenly she didn't care about her outfit or her shoes. Instead she continued hurling insults at me, stepping into the running water of the hydrant as she did.

Mom was way down at the other end of the block when the incident took place, but when some of the other kids ran to tell her that the lady was screaming at me, she raced to my defense.

She pulled the woman away from me. "If you're gonna smack anyone, bitch, smack me!" Mom snarled. The expression on her face would have terrified a prizefighter.

Suddenly the woman wasn't so brave. Without saying a word, she picked up her grocery bags then climbed the steps to her house. From that day forward, whenever I was playing outside and that lady saw me, she crossed the street and walked on the other side.

It was possible that my mother was remembering the incident as Aunt Mary was talking to her because I saw her expression change. They exchanged a few more words in Sicilian (they did that whenever they didn't want the kids to know what they were saying), then suddenly Mom's anger was turned on me. "Go outside, Tisha," was all she said as she walked away.

At that moment I felt betrayed. I hated Aunt Mary. Of course she would know what food was fattening and what food wasn't because like my grandmother, Aunt Mary had dieted herself up to wearing a size twenty-six housecoat.

I ran upstairs and flung myself onto my Aunt Santa's bed. When my mother came after me she tried to explain the situation. "Aunt Mary is worried about you and she's right. Do you want to grow up to be as fat as she is?"

No one wanted me to be fat—least of all me. But I was fat! It was strange that the very adults who had been demanding that I eat so other children didn't starve were now blaming me for my lack of self-control and for my obesity.

The whole situation was very confusing.

That night I cried myself to sleep and a few days later I was introduced to dieting by the diet gurus themselves . . . Grandma Blackie and Aunt Mary.

Between the two of them, they had tried every diet known to man. They tried the "Grapefruit Diet" where they ate anything they wanted as long as it was preceded by the consumption of half a grapefruit. The "Cabbage Diet" where they put all the food they planned to eat for the day into a pot with cabbage and boiled it so they could eat it as soup. The "Hot Dog Diet"—the "Peanut Butter Diet"—and the "Milkshake Diet". They even tried a diet where they ate these little chocolate candies with a cup of hot water before each meal. It was supposed to be an appetite suppressant, but for them it was more like a treat.

My first diet was one they secretly drafted me into. Needless to say, it failed, but it was kind of fun.

My father, who at the time was studying to be a Buddhist Monk (did I mention that I grew up in the seventies?) came home one day and announced to the family that he was going to cleanse his system by ingesting nothing but water for three days. It would, he told us, purify his body and open up his mind to accept spirituality. Upon hearing that at the end of his three-day fast my father lost ten pounds, Grandma Blackie and Aunt Mary decided this was just the thing they needed to drop some weight so they would look good for an upcoming wedding.(Since I was staying with my grandmother for a few days I was sucked into their little plan.)

After much consideration the diet gurus decided that the "Water Diet" as they called it, would work better if it included exercise. They devised a routine whereby we would run (I hobbled because of my brace) up the stairs then into the bedroom jiggling our fat until we worked up a good sweat. We did this every half hour or so.

They also decided that the key to the diet's success was to monitor our water intake. You see, we didn't want to consume more water than we sweated out because this, they concluded, would cause us to gain "water weight". One needed to be very conscious of "water weight" because it could strike when least expected and possibly stand in the way of the stunning figures we were sure to obtain at the end of this 72-hour program.

Exactly three hours into the diet, starvation set in. No matter how hard I tried I couldn't take my mind off the fact that I needed something to eat. Apparently the diet gurus felt the same way because each time they passed the refrigerator they got a bit closer to it.

"I need some water," Grandma Blackie barked. "Anybody want some?"

"I'll have a glass," Aunt Mary said as she gave into temptation and unwittingly opened the refrigerator door.

"Shut the fridge and come over here," Grandma snapped. "You can't have anything to eat!"

"I know, I know," Mary replied.

"Then what were you doing? Letting all the cold air out?"

"I was just looking," Mary said as she took a seat in between Grandma and me at the kitchen table.

There was a long silence and suddenly I felt very uncomfortable. This wasn't the Grandma Blackie's house that I knew where everyone spoke at once while the smell of frying garlic wafted through the air. Instead it was a sad, quite place like my friend Joanie McCarthy's house where everyone's manners were as polished as the furniture and the fruit on the table was only for looking because it was made of wax.

We quietly sipped our water trying not to think about food when Aunt Mary had an epiphany. "Why can't we put some lemon in our water?" she asked out loud. "If the acid in grapefruit burns fat faster then why can't lemon do the same? It has just as much acid as grapefruit."

Grandma considered this for a moment. Lemons did have as much acid as grapefruit so if we put some lemon juice into our water it would burn our fat faster and make us feel full. We all agreed that this made good sense so we added lemon to our tap water.

The only thing the lemon did was make the water too bitter to drink. We looked to the chef among us for a solution and true to form, Grandma had one right off the top of her head. She got up from the table and pulled a plastic tube of saccharin out of the cabinet then plopped a couple of white tablets into each of our water glasses. We all sipped and I made a face. The saccharin made the water taste nasty.

The gurus deliberated further until they finally decided that a spoonful of sugar was the only thing that would make the water drinkable. The added caloric intake, they deduced, would be negated by all the stair running and fat shaking we were doing.

So we drank our water with lemon and sugar then did a few more laps up the stairs. Crisis averted. We were all back on track.

Another hour passed and we were starving again. The collective stomach grumbling sounded as if the "N" train was running right through the basement kitchen. It was clear we needed to eat something but no one wanted to break the "diet." We had done so well up until that point.

It was my grandmother who spoke up, declaring that if grapefruit burned enough calories for someone to create a diet around it then it stood to reason that eating grapefruit on the "Water Diet" would move the fat burning process along more quickly. After all, we were burning all those extra calories running up and down the stairs and shaking our fat—the grapefruit would give us energy to keep on going.

It was agreed—grapefruit became part of the "Water Diet."

We each took half a grapefruit and gazed upon it as if it were a scrumptious plate of pasta. My grandmother took a bite. This time she made a face. The grapefruit had been sitting in the house since the failed "Grapefruit Diet" and now it was quite bitter. "We can't eat it like this," she said.

Aunt Mary and I watched her as she pushed her chair from the table and headed for the same cabinet where she kept the saccharin. We both wondered what the great diet guru would do next.

Grandma again brought down the white ceramic sugar bowl and sprinkled each of our grapefruit halves with a teaspoon of sugar. Pleased with herself, she sat back down and we all enjoyed our grapefruit without uttering a word.

Sugar was quickly becoming part of the "Water Diet".

By mid-day we all felt fatigued. I'm not certain if it was physical fatigue from hobbling up and down the stairs shaking my fat, or mental fatigue from trying to figure out ways to make this diet work better, but either way, we were pooped.

We needed some type of nutrition and it was up to Grandma to figure out how we could be nourished without breaking the diet. She remembered reading somewhere that celery was so low in calories that a person burned more chewing it than it actually contained. (That made me wonder why people on diets didn't just eat celery all day but I didn't ask the question because I was afraid I'd get in trouble.) Grandma pulled three celery stalks out of the fridge, washed them and sprinkled each with salt. Celery was now part of the "Water Diet."

We happily crunched our celery and consumed just the right amount of water to replace that which we sweated out without gaining any "water weight". We were happy—that is until Aunt Mary decided she needed a cup of coffee if she was going to have enough energy to run up those stairs one more time.

"It'll be okay if we drink it black," she said to my Grandmother who readily agreed. But black tasted awful and so they broke out the white ceramic sugar bowl once again and went to the refrigerator for the cream. Since I was too young for coffee they let me drink a small glass of cola.

We were chatting away about the upcoming wedding and how wonderful we would all look when Grandma, naturally and without thought, opened up the Tupperware container filled with the sesame seed cookies she had baked in case company dropped by. We all reached for one.

"This diet isn't so bad," said Aunt Mary in between bites. She looked down at the table where several sesame seeds had escaped her lips. She picked them up with her fingertips then sucked them into her mouth. "How much weight do you think we'll lose?" she asked in between nibbles.

"Well," Grandma said, dunking her cookie into her coffee. I scrunched up my face. Though I come from a family of dunkers, I am a purist, preferring not to mix my food with liquid of any sort. Grandma kept on talking, "Tony lost ten pounds and he really isn't fat at all."

She looked at me as she imparted her next bit of wisdom. "The more weight you have to lose the faster it comes off." I nodded as if I understood this. She continued, "If he lost ten pounds then that's a little more than three pounds a day." She reached for another cookie. Aunt Mary and I followed her lead. "If he had anything to lose at all it was those ten pounds right?"

Aunt Mary nodded because her mouth was full of cookie and she didn't want another morsel to escape. I too was nodding. Nodding as I reached across the table to take another cookie.

My grandmother's eyes narrowed and I jerked my hand back before she could smack it. She continued, "We have about ten times more weight to lose than Tony did." She stopped talking then closed her eyes for a moment to do the math in her head. She was smiling when she opened her eyes again. "If we have ten times more to lose than he did and he lost ten, I would say we could expect to lose thirty pounds or so."

Thirty pounds in seventy two hours! These women were brilliant!

I tried to do the math in my own head but I wasn't up to that level in school yet. Aunt Mary, on the other hand, nodded her agreement then doled out another cookie to each of us. She put the container back on the counter with the rest of the bread and pastry items always available in the house.

Grandma kept her house well stocked for "company". For the grandchildren she kept ice cream, cones and sprinkles as well as a variety of the good cereals like "Cocoa Puffs and "Fruit Loops." There was also a never-ending supply of potato chips stashed around the place—this due to the fact that my uncle Vinny loved salt.

Time seemed to pass more easily after our cookie break. Aunt Mary said it was because our bodies were getting used to the starvation. We continued our stair jogging and fat shaking until it was time to make dinner for those lucky people in the house who weren't on diets.

That night's menu consisted of fried veal cutlets, mashed potatoes and salad with lemon and oil dressing. As the smell of the frying cutlets wafted through the house, I went to the sink to refill my glass of water. Grandma was eating one of the very small pieces of veal cutlet that broke off in the pan (that's when I learned that there are no calories in broken pieces of food). She made a face then turned to look at me. "Taste this," she said as she sawed off a piece from a bigger cutlet then placed it in a paper towel to sop up the excess oil. "Does this taste right to you?"

I looked at the cutlet and my mouth watered. I really wanted to eat it but something was stopping me. I thought about the diet and how my father did it. When he was fasting he didn't eat anything. No lemon, no celery, no grapefruit, certainly no cookies. Somehow I didn't think the cutlet was "allowed" on this diet.

On the other hand, my father didn't know half as much about dieting as these women did. In my short lifetime they must have lost more than a hundred pounds each on their various diets. I distinctly remember them announcing a twenty-pound loss here or a thirty-pound loss there. Surely they were diet experts. Who was I to question whether this cutlet, which was causing me to drool, was allowed on the "Water Diet"? Besides, this wasn't the same type of diet my father had been on. These women had already vastly improved it with their endless stream of nutritional knowledge.

I shoved the piece of cutlet into my mouth. "Tastes great!" I exclaimed through clamped lips. I didn't want to lose one delectable crumb.

"I don't know," she said as she sliced another piece for herself. "It tastes flat."

One thing you should know about my grandmother-though she was a fabulous cook, her taste buds were burned beyond repair by her need to douse everything in hot sauce. She was always complaining that her gravy was "agita" (bitter) or the cheese in the lasagna tasted "spoilt" (sour). Hence she needed to taste everything she was cooking over and over again.

"Mary," she bellowed as she sawed another cutlet in half. "Taste this and tell me if you think it is flat."

Never one to argue with her older sister, Mary tasted the cutlet. "It tastes fine, Angie." She shoved the other half in her mouth then turned to run up the stairs and shake her fat again.

"You want some water," I said, holding out the glass I had just filled from the tap.

"No," she replied, "but I'll have another cup of coffee if you don't mind making it for me."

I poured the coffee from the electric percolator and set it on the kitchen table then took a seat so I could watch the old black and white television that was stowed amidst the bread and pastries. Grandma continued grumbling. Now she was going on about how the salad was too salty. Aunt Mary yelled to her from her place on the stairs, "If they make sangwitches (sandwiches) out of the cutlets and the salad then no one will notice if it's salty."

My grandmother's eyes lit up. She grabbed a loaf of Italian bread from among the half dozen on the counter and sliced it lengthwise. She scraped out the soft dough in the center so there would be enough room to fill the crusty bread with salad. On top of this she laid several cutlets. She sliced the sandwich into strips, put them on three plates and brought the plates over to the table where I was sipping my water with lemon. The lemon really was a good idea because I was starting to feel full.

"Here," she said as she slid a plate toward me. "Try this."

I did as she commanded and told her it tasted delicious. Mary quickly took the seat next to mine. She dunked the tip of her sandwich into her coffee (lots of cream and three sugars) then bit into it. I scrunched my face. The oil from the cutlet left a film on top of the coffee. "Its fine, Angie," she said as she took another bite.

Grandma finished her sandwich but I could tell by the expression on her face that she still wasn't satisfied. She hoisted her girth up from the table to slice some more of the sandwich then brought the pieces back to the table.

We all chewed thoughtfully, telling her between bites how delicious it tasted.

"You just think so because we are starving to death from this diet."

The diet! By then I was certain that we weren't doing it exactly right. We barely drank any water since the coffee break and our exercise was repeatedly being interrupted by our eating.

Panicked, I pushed myself from the table and filled three glasses with tap water, hoping that we could absolve ourselves by drinking it. (Did I mention that I'm a Catholic?)

"None for me," said Aunt Mary who had poured herself another cup of coffee and was now reopening the Tupperware container of cookies.

My grandmother took the glass I offered her then went to the sink to dump it out so she could fill it with Coke. "Open the cabinet and grab the potato chips, bella," she said as she retook her place at the table.

It was clear that this diet was doomed to failure but since I was too young to argue, I happily went along for the ride.

When we were finished eating I cleaned the table and set it for my grandfather, aunts, uncles and parents who were all arriving for dinner. While they ate Aunt Mary, Grandma and I sat in our seats sipping our water with lemon.

I felt guilty and it must have shown on my face because my mother looked at me curiously. "What's the matter with you?" she asked, her eyes squinting to let me know she was about to answer her own question. "Don't tell me that you've been fasting with these two all day."

I opened my mouth to answer but it was too late. She issued a laser beam glare at my grandmother and aunt then turned her full ire on the poor man who brought this preposterous concept home to us.

"Do you see what you did, Tony? I can't believe you! Fasting! Really!" These words were issued in little puffs as my mother heaped food onto the empty plate in front of my father then reached across him to hand it to me.

Concern immediately marked my father's face. "How do you feel, sweetheart?" he asked as he stroked my cheek with the back of his hand. "Are you dizzy or anything?" I shook my head and he continued, "Well, I think your mother is right. Fasting isn't about losing weight it's about cleansing your body. You are too young for this."

He grabbed the plate from my mother then shoved it under my nose. "I want you to eat something right now, okay?"

I looked at Grandma and Aunt Mary, feeling like I would betray them if I ate the food, but Grandma nodded at me. "Go ahead and eat. I've been rethinking this whole thing anyway and I'm not sure it is very healthy."

She extracted more plates and silverware from the various drawers and cabinets where she kept them then passed a setting to Aunt Mary.

We all feasted on veal cutlets, mashed potatoes, salad and Italian bread. For dessert we had sesame cookies and ice cream.

Though my first attempt at dieting was a failure my future held many more opportunities to get it right.

CHAPTER THREE

Pool Daze

When I was eleven-years-old my parents announced that we were moving to Florida. My brother and I couldn't believe our luck. We were going to be living in the "Sunshine State"—the home of Disney World, Sea World and endless summers. We would swim, fish and play outside no matter what month it was. It was going to be terrific.

My father's parents, Grandma and Grandpa Albert, had moved there the year before and I missed them terribly. I had lived with them for a couple of years when I was in Kindergarten and first grade. Because of my Leg Perthes Disease, I needed to be in a "special" classroom. The only public school that offered the option was right down the block from their house so that's where I lived. Apparently they missed us too because they bought us the house next door so we could be near them. There was a canal in the backyard where we could fish from our very own dock. There were orange and grapefruit trees all over our property. We even had our very own coconut tree.

Yes siree, Florida had everything a kid could want—unless that kid was a fat, Italian from New York City. It didn't take me long to find out that Florida wasn't all I thought it would be.

The heat and humidity was oppressive for a kid carrying an extra hundred pounds. Most days I had to change my clothes three or four times because I sweat right through them.

The only place there was to go swimming was at the public pool nearly a mile away. Since my father hadn't found steady employment, we didn't have enough money for bicycles so we had to walk in the unbearable heat. Once we got to the pool the real fun began.

Because we were Italian, my brother and I stood out like sore thumbs. We were the only dark haired, dark eyed kids at the pool. To make matters worse, I was clearly the fattest person (adult or child) who dared to darken the doorstep of the Sunrise Boulevard Pool. I was eleven-years-old and weighed two-hundred-twenty-five pounds and I had the nerve to show up to the pool wearing a bikini.

You may wonder why someone of my size would even own a bikini. Looking back-I wonder too. All I can tell you is that I owned one and wore it. I didn't even have the good taste to wear a long shirt over it while I swam like some of the other kids who had ten ounces of baby fat to hide.

No. Not me. I had nothing to hide. Every member of my family told me that I was the most beautiful girl in the world. That even though I was a bit chubby I had a very pretty face. If I was certain of anything it was that I had everything under control.

So there I was, a kinky haired, brown eyed, broad nosed, Italian girl confident in the fact that the six inches of material covering her fifty inch ass was a perfectly acceptable outfit to go swimming in. Boy was I wrong.

Anyone who has ever been a teenager, known a teenager or raised a teenager knows that they are meaner than any junkyard dog and as vicious as wolves if they collect in packs. In Florida they collected in blonde-haired, blue-eyed packs led by the king and queen of the local high school.

The moment I showed up at the pool they descended on me like flies to road kill, shouting things like "Blimp" and "Beached Whale." They showed me no mercy. Even the kids who were the usual targets of the "in crowd's" assaults, zeroed in on me.

Once again I was the center of attention but this time I was sorry for it. They weren't focusing on me because I was a good, little girl who cleaned her plate so that other kids didn't starve or because I was the only student in class who knew the right answer consistently. They were focusing on me because I was a fat, Italian kid who had the nerve to go swimming in "their" pool wearing a bikini.

When my brother and I finally left the pool that first day, the bikini wasn't the only thing I was wearing—I was also wearing the left over ice cream and chewed up Starbursts flung at me by the native kids.

I was mortified. These kids were animals. It was clear that I couldn't step foot inside that pool again so I made up my mind, swore an oath and resigned myself to stick to it. I was never going back to that pool again. My brother, however, had other ideas.

Every day he begged me to take him to the pool and every day I refused because I was scared of those nasty teenagers. I could see the disappointment in his face and I felt like a heel. My poor little brother, the light of my life, had to suffer because his sister was a coward.

Well the one thing I learned from growing up in a matriarchal family was that no one can defeat us when we are willing to fight.

Women in my family have done some amazing things. For instance, Grandma Blackie's father died when she was a child and she practically raised Aunt Mary on her own. During World War II, Grandma Albert got trapped in Naples while my grandfather was in America trying to earn enough money to bring the family over. My uncles and father were all under ten-years-old at the time so it was up to Grandma and her three sisters to figure out ways to feed, clothe and protect the entire family from the Nazi soldiers who were occupying the village.

If these two women could face down death, despair and German soldiers then the least I could do was stand up to a bunch of teenagers so my baby brother could go swimming.

One week later I donned one of my father's "t" shirts, which happened to be a bit snug on me, put a dollar worth of quarters in the pocket, grabbed a couple of towels and my brother's hand then marched down to the pool ready to do battle.

Little did I know that the first person I would have to battle with was Annie, the pool's gate keeper. Annie was a forty-something woman who wore green eye shadow and teased her platinum blonde hair high to cover the bald spot at the back of her head. She was the only person who could sell you Jujubes and give you access to the pool.

There were two ways to get into the pool. Either you bought a yearly membership and Annie kept your card on file or you paid fifty cents at the window as a one-time user and Annie decided whether or not you got in based upon how many regular members were already swimming in the pool that day. You see, regular membership guaranteed you entrance to the pool but the "fifty cents" people, like my brother and me, were totally at Annie's mercy. She was "the law"—period—end of story.

I approached Annie's window with caution. She had a Benson and Hedges 100's cigarette hanging out of the corner of her mouth (I know what kind of cigarette it was because later in the story I'll be swiping one from her). I knew Annie had witnessed what happened to me the week before, but like Bob the lifeguard, a young, handsome, athletically built man who drove an orange MGB Midget, she ignored it.

Annie saw me coming. She lifted her ashtray up onto the counter then leaned out the window a bit as I dug into the pocket of my father's too tight shirt to come up with the coins for admission. As I struggled to pull the last quarter from my pocket, Annie said in her lovely Southern drawl, "Sorry, Sweetie, but the pool's full up today."

Full? I turned around to look. The pool was nearly empty. The adult swim class that took place from 10 AM to 11 AM had vacated long ago. The lifeguards had all taken their lunch breaks and were now seated on their tall chairs. In fact, the only people in the pool were the same nasty kids from the week before.

Maybe my Great Aunt Mary did have a point about me needing to learn how to act like a child and not hang around with adults so much because what I did next was apparently unacceptable behavior in "the South".

I set my jaw and clenched my fists before stating in my heavy New York accent, "But there's nobody in there."

Annie's eyes narrowed and she leaned over the counter until she was sure I would hear her. "Listen c' here, you disrespectful child."

She was furious. It was bad enough that someone questioned her authority—it was worse that the "someone" was a kid—a fat, Italian, Yankee kid at that.

She drew on her cigarette then let the smoke roll out of her mouth and stream from her nostrils before she continued, "I say what goes c' here! I decide who gets into that pool! If I have a mind to, I can ban your butt for a year. Or forever! Don't y'all ever question me again. Got it?"

I nodded my head slowly, utterly amazed that there was an adult in the world who didn't instantly fall in love with me. Who didn't realize how good I was. I wasn't the type of kid to give anyone trouble. All my teachers said I was the perfect little girl (although I talked too much). I did all my homework, ate all my food so children wouldn't starve. I went to church every day and confession once a week. I was as smart as many adults (my father told me so). So why then didn't this woman like me?

"What ch'all waiting for?" Annie asked. Her nostrils were still smoking. She looked like a dragon. She waved her hand toward the exit. "Go on, git!"

I walked away wondering what I had done to make her so mad. I didn't tell my parents about it because I felt ashamed.

That night I offered to clear the table. I had already eaten my dinner and my mother wouldn't allow me to have seconds, so I pretended to scrape the plates but instead ate the food my brother left on his plate as well as a measured portion of all the leftovers so my mother wouldn't notice that I had been eating after she told me not to.

For every remaining day of that summer I donned my father's too tight "t" shirt, shoved fifty cents into the front pocket, grabbed a towel and headed down to the pool. Every day I was refused admittance. Annie did let my brother in. She had no problem with him because he hadn't "sassed" her like I did. I, on the other hand, was banned until further notice.

I wasn't sure what "sassed" meant but I figured it was something like talking back. I hardly believed that it was the only reason she banned me from the pool.

Since my brother wasn't old enough to stay at the pool alone, I spent my time waiting for him talking with Annie at the candy counter. I used my fifty cents on Sugar Straws, Now and Laters and Jelly Fish. I never bought the good stuff like M&M's or Hershey bars. It wasn't that I didn't like chocolate—I loved it, but chocolate bars were the most expensive candies. I got more for my money with the sugar candy.

One day while moving around the inside of her stand filling my order, Annie asked me, "How come y'all eat so much candy? Don't cha know that sugar makes y'all fat?"

Of course I knew that sugar made "me" fat, unlike the rest of the kids who could eat sugar all day and never gain an ounce.

"I know," I said as I looked down at my shuffling feet. "My mother says I have big bones and a slow metabolism. I can't really exercise because of my hip."

"Oh," Annie said, suspiciously. "What's wrong with y'all's hip?"

I explained that I was diagnosed with Leg Perthes Disease and from age three to age nine I had to wear a brace on my leg which kept me inactive.

"I can't move very well so my body doesn't have as much energy as other kids. That's why I'm fat."

"Oh, really?" Again, Annie sounded suspicious. "Can I tell y'all sum'un?"

Annie was the gatekeeper for the pool. She could tell me whatever she wanted as long as it meant that someday she would let me back in the pool.

"I think that the reason y'all are so fat is 'cause ya eats too much. I understand about your leg and all, and I'm sure it had sum'un to do with y'all putting on weight, but I see how much junk y'all eat hangin 'round c' here. If y'all was my kid I would put cha on a diet insteada letting y'all do this to yourself."

Her words hurt and it must have shown in my face because she leaned over the counter and said, "Sweetie, come ova c' here." When I did, she continued in a low voice, "I didn't say that to hurt y'all, I said it to help. I know what it's like to be fat. I was a very fat teenager."

You could have knocked me over with a feather. It was hard to believe that Annie was ever more than a few pounds overweight.

She nodded her head as if she could read my thoughts then said, "Why do y'all think I won't let cha back in the pool? It's not because I don't like y'all. It's because I know that those kids are gonna torture ya about your weight. I don't want to see that happen to nobody—'specially on my watch. I don't want any trouble c' here and I sure as heck can't control the nastiness that comes out of the mouths of them there young'uns. So I figure the best way to protect y'all is to ban your butt."

"I really would like to go swimming," I replied, offering her the most pathetic expression I could muster. "It's hot out here and I have to wait for my brother anyway. If you let me in I promise not to start any trouble."

Annie looked at me. I knew she would take pity on me. I was sweating enough to soak through Dad's shirt. "Y'all mean you're jes gonna let them call y'all names and not get angry?" she asked, disbelief heavy in her voice. "I heard that Eyetalians from New Yawk have very bad tempers. I don't want no trouble c' here."

I wanted to laugh at that statement but I was afraid that Annie would think I was laughing at her. Italians from New York did have bad tempers judging from my mother and her sisters, but I was too insecure to get angry with anyone-yet.

"I won't start any trouble," I promised her, and meant it. "If they tease me, I promise I'll walk away."

"Will y'all keep your shirt on while you're swimmin so they won't have much to talk about?"

"Absolutely!" I had already taken a good look at myself in the mirror and realized that I never wanted to expose that much skin again.

"Well," Annie said, snuffing out her cigarette in the ashtray. She picked up the rubber stamp that marked the hands of fifty cents people "PAID" then she waved me closer. "Give me your hand. Y'all can pay me tomorrow, okay?"

"Okay," I agreed before making my way down the concrete hallway that smelled of chlorine to emerge at the edge of the pool.

The "in crowd" were too busy talking to each other to notice me walking onto the pool deck to find a chair. For that I was grateful. I scanned the expanse of the Olympic sized pool in search of my brother. He was playing with a group of boys about his age at the low end.

I laid my towel down on a chair then quickly made my way to the edge of the pool so I could jump in before anyone noticed me. Once I was in the water, I knew my body wouldn't be so offensive.

The water was so refreshing that I instantly felt less anxious. I sank all the way down until my feet hit the floor then propelled my way up to the top again. When my head broke through the water I realized that everyone was laughing. I quickly checked my top but remembered that I was wearing a "t" shirt. I checked my nose for stray boogers but it was clean. I couldn't imagine what they were laughing at.

I turned my head to see if they might be laughing at someone else. Then I saw it. Bob, the incredibly handsome lifeguard, had been standing behind me about to ascend his chair when I jumped in. The splash I made was so large that it soaked him. He stood there with arms and legs akimbo, dripping wet and waiting for me to resurface. I was mortified.

"Hey, kid," he said as he picked up my towel and dried himself off. "Next time you want to jump in the pool use the stairs. Got it?"

He threw my towel back on my chair then climbed the ladder to his perch. I could hear whispers of "Whale" as I got out of the pool. My brother and I left immediately.

CHAPTER FOUR

The Fat Girl's Revenge

For a long time I tried to avoid the pool entirely. My brother and I swam in the canal behind our house but we caught impetigo and had to stop. We had an old row boat that we filled with water and sat in but it wasn't any fun. Finally I gave in to his whining and brought him back to the pool.

While Albert was swimming I passed the time talking with Annie. She told me all about how she lost weight counting calories and how she was now an expert at knowing the caloric value of ordinary food. I told her about the "Water Diet" and we both had a good laugh. Occasionally, when there weren't too many teenagers in the pool, I would go swimming but mostly I just hung out in the cool, concrete hallway.

It turned out that hanging out with Annie was the best thing I could have done. When the kids came up to the window Annie would introduce me and tell them that I was her friend. It was her personal seal of approval. The kids understood that if they gave me any trouble they would have to answer to her-and nobody wanted to have to answer to Annie. Soon kids were asking me to hang out with them in the pool. Spot them while they did handstands or be on their team during Marco Polo (I was always the bottom guy). Soon after I began night swimming with the teenagers and even made friends with the sister of a cheerleader who happened to live next door to us. Her name was Sharon Krauss and her blonde-haired, blue-eyed, big-chested, cheerleader sister's name was Pam.

Sharon and I became best friends. She taught me how to twirl a baton and how to do handstands. We were very active and it began showing in my waistline. I didn't lose much weight, just enough so that Dad's shirt wasn't so tight anymore.

Florida was finally living up to its promise. I was making friends and enjoying life. Even my little brother seemed to be less of a pain in the neck. Those last weeks of summer were among the best days of my life-until the night when I got banned from the pool for good.

It was a night just like any other. Sharon and her boyfriend, Michael Fields (a tall, blonde football player with sea green eyes and golden skin everywhere the sun kissed it) were snuggling on the stairs. As usual, I was hanging out by myself on the other side of the pool daydreaming that it was me who Michael was snuggling. Out of nowhere Sharon's sister, Pam broke away from her cheerleader friends and came marching down the deck to poke me in the head with her toe.

"What are you looking at?" she demanded.

"Nothing," I replied, utterly confused as to why she would be so angry with me.

"I saw y'all looking at my sister and her boyfriend. You want to trade places with her, don'tcha?"

I was absolutely mortified. Had she read my mind? I tried not to be obvious with my stare but somehow Pam knew that I liked Michael. How could that be? The only person who knew how much I liked Michael Fields was my mother and she certainly couldn't have said anything.

"I don't know what you're talking about," I said as I moved away from the edge of the pool so Pam would stop poking me with her pink polished toes. She jumped in.

"Admit it," she said as she shoved my shoulders. "Admit that you want Michael to be your boyfriend. Admit that y'all are only pretending to be my sister's friend. Admit that you're a greasy, fat Eyetalian pig who would steal her best friend's boyfriend."

She was pushing me hard and I stumbled back into Sharon and Michael who were watching with interest.

When I bumped into Sharon, she unleashed on me. "You think you can steal my boyfriend?" she asked, looking me over as if I were a piece of trash.

"She's so fat and greasy that she's leaving an oil slick on the pool," Pam yelled out. "She couldn't steal anyone's boyfriend."

They were both yelling at me, accusing me of being a traitor and a bad person. It was true that I thought Michael was cute. Every girl did—but I wasn't the type of girl who could flirt with a boy. For crying out loud, I barely had enough confidence to form a friendship with a girl let alone a good-looking guy like Michael Fields.

"Why don't you admit that you've been plotting to make Sharon look bad so Michael would dump her," Pam screeched. "Admit it because your mom told my mom all about it."

My face must have shown my shock because at that point everyone started laughing, even Michael Fields. How could my mother do such a thing? When she noticed I had lost some weight she asked me if there was a boy who I liked. I told her that I thought Michael was cute. I never

Dreamed she would tell Sharon's mother about it. What was she thinking?

Somehow I got sandwiched between Pam and Sharon. Pam was so close that I could smell the alcohol on her breath. "Well?" she asked, her face smug with the knowledge that she was utterly destroying me.

"Let me pass," I shouted as she weaved side to side, blocking my path to the stairs. She tried to grab me but I slipped through her grasp.

She's so greasy that I can't even get a hold of her," she called out to her friends who all exploded with another burst of laughter.

I climbed the stairs, grabbed my towel then marched through the tunnel and out into the park. I could hear them following me. Pam was calling out names but she must have stumbled on her own feet because suddenly the footsteps stopped and I could hear people asking if she was okay.

I was just outside the gate when I heard someone running up behind me. It was Sharon. She was still dripping wet in her orange bikini. She called my name then ran forward and jumped onto my back. I felt her knuckles strike the side of my head. She whooped and yelled until I tossed her onto the black top at my feet.

Seeing this, Pam came running forward in a blaze of blonde hair and boobs. She was taller than me but definitely not bigger. She charged me with her teeth bared, fully intending to bite me.

At first I didn't know what to do but then my instincts kicked in. I pushed Pam aside with my palm to her chin. Her mouth slammed shut and she broke her front tooth.

"Bitch," she barked, the air whistling through her broken tooth. Then she tried to kick me but I grabbed her foot and flipped her over.

It was a good thing that she was a cheerleader because she went with the motion and landed on her feet. This impressed the gathered crowd. Their approval bolstered her.

She came at me again. This time she tried to punch me in the stomach. I grabbed her by the hair and brought my knee up into her groin. Then I yanked her hair so hard it came out in clumps in my hand. Next, I slapped her face, causing her nose to bleed. I don't know how many more times I hit her or where. All I know is that by the time I was finished she was a sobbing heap on the ground and her tidy, white bathing suit was streaked with her own blood.

It was Michael Fields who pulled me off her. He told me that I needed to stop hitting her before I killed her. Suddenly my senses returned. I slipped off Pam then moved slowly to where I dropped my towel and picked it up.

By this time, Bob the lifeguard had emerged from the pool area and into the parking lot. It was dark except for the streetlights. Pam was lying flat on her back and Bob stooped down to check her out. She was bleeding pretty badly from her nose. Bob ran back to get the first aid kit then began ministering to her while the other kids looked on.

I was waiting for the light to change so I could cross the street when I heard footsteps behind me. Fearing that it might be Sharon seeking to avenge her sister, I turned abruptly, ready for another fight. It was Michael Fields.

At first I flinched. I didn't know what he was going to do to me. Then I noticed the slight smile on his face. "Man, you really kicked her ass good! You okay?"

I looked down at my hands. My knuckles were red from where Pam's teeth cut into them but other than that I was okay.

"Yeah," I said.

The light had changed so I began to cross the street. Michael reached out and grabbed my hand. "I'll call you tomorrow. Maybe we can hang out some time." He flashed his bright, white smile.

I don't remember much after that. My hand was warm and tingly from where he touched me and my head was fuzzy. All I could think about the whole way home was that Michael Fields wanted to hang out with me.

Michael called me the next day and nearly every day after that. We never did become boyfriend and girlfriend but we were friends all the same. He invited me to his football games and to hang out with him and the other guys when they practiced in the park. When Sharon found out that we were friends, she dumped him and told everyone that he was in love with me. That made Michael uncomfortable. After a while he stopped asking me to hang out.

I was sad about losing Michael as a friend, but by that time my reputation as the crazy Yankee who whipped Pam Krauss' ass was well established. Soon I had more friends than I could handle. Guys and girls who were tired of being abused by the "in crowd" and transplanted northerners who felt more comfortable with one of their own than with the blonde-haired, blue-eyed Floridians, all wanted to be my friend. Then there were the geeks—dozens of them. I was a geek magnet. They looked to me for protection and I happily gave it to them.

My reputation as a good girl totally disappeared. It was replaced by this new, powerful one. It wasn't exactly what I had hoped for but at least I had friends.

***Update—The Krauss girls eventually moved to the next town. It was called Coconut Creek, a very upscale community that was home to the new high school. The next time I saw them was while I was attending that school. I was a hundred pounds thinner due to some whacky diet tactics that I will describe in the next chapter. I looked pretty good and I am happy to report that I ultimately succeeded in stealing both their boyfriends.

CHAPTER FIVE

Bulimia, Diet Pills and
Other Teenage Stuff

The late seventies were all about disco, being thin and partying. So it only made sense that diet pills were readily available.

I managed to get through most of Junior High School without incident thanks to my reputation as a crazy, fat, Eyetalian who beat the ass of a High School cheerleader. People were so frightened of me that I was able to collect my own group of misfits who I protected with my all-encompassing power. If you were a nerd, geek, pimply or hairy, you got to be part of my gang and were automatically respected by all.

It was during that time when I met Nikki and Lori Mazy-two girls who are my closest friends until this day. They moved to Florida from Michigan. Nikki was a chubby ten-year-old who had skipped a grade in school because she was so smart. Her older sister, Lori was skinny but her Hungarian heritage was obvious by the amount of dark hair covering her arms and legs. Lori and Nikki lived right down the street from me so we took the same school bus. That's where I first met them.

Dawn was just breaking as I groggily made my way down the road to the Tenneco station where the school bus picked us up. I wasn't paying much attention to things because like most twelve-year-olds, I had barely gotten any sleep the night before. It was a day just like any other except for the fact that the natives were growling as they gathered around something outside the store. As I got closer I realized that the blue-eyed, blonde-haired pack was preparing to eat Lori and Nikki alive.

It was clear that the new kids needed help so I sprang into action. I used my girth to push through the crowd. Lori and Nikki's eyes opened wide when they saw me coming toward them. "Back off!" I barked to the kids surrounding them. "They belong to me!"

Everyone backed up but no one scattered. They all wanted to see what the crazy Eyetalian was going to do with the new kids.

Lori and Nikki were scared to death. Nikki may have even wet her pants. "Come on," I commanded as the bus rolled to a stop in front of us. I headed toward the door. "In the back with me!"

My new found power gave me the right to claim the entire back seat of the bus for myself even if it meant that the other kids had to sit three to a bench. Lori wasn't sure what to do. She hesitated for a moment but Nikki followed. She must have figured that I would show them some type of ethnic courtesy. She was right.

When I got them to the back of the bus I introduced myself and told them all about the neighborhood. I assured them that if they stuck with me the natives wouldn't bother them. To be sure that they believed me, I told them the story about how I beat Pam Krauss' ass. I could see that they became less nervous. "If we stick together," I told them, turning suddenly to glare at one of the boys who was studying us. He immediately turned around. "If we stick together," I continued, "then we'll be even stronger."

It was at that moment that we formed a lifelong bond. From that day on our singular focus was to make ourselves thin and beautiful so that we could become the "in crowd".

We looked each other over and considered what we needed to do to create this transformation. For Lori it was easy. All she needed was a bottle of Nair and some new clothes. For me and Nikki the transformation was going to be a bit harder because we needed to stop eating.

Since walking was good exercise and exercise was a great start to a diet, we all began walking around the neighborhood after school and after dinner. Every day we walked from our house to the Tenneco station at the end of the main road and back again. That was about a mile. We walked a little over a mile to the pool but never went swimming. We decided that swimming was for chumps so instead we hung out by the window with Annie and on occasion, I swiped a cigarette from her because we heard that smoking suppressed the appetite.

When we weren't walking, we were babysitting. We liked babysitting because we earned the money for Nair, new clothes and over the counter diet pills. The exercise we got running after the kids was a huge bonus.

The weight started coming off slowly, but it was coming off. The more I lost, the more I wanted to lose. Soon I began skipping breakfast. This took the weight off faster. When I noticed how well that worked I started skipping lunch. Instead I spent my lunch hour sitting alone reading. This aloof behavior furthered my reputation as a dangerous character—it also helped to elevate me to Honor Student.

Nikki lost her weight far more quickly than I lost mine. Hers was mostly baby fat and as soon as she got her period it came off. I, on the other hand, continued to struggle. Our neighborhood walks soon became the subject of discussion among the "in crowd". The hair on Lori's head was long and luxurious and the hair on her arms had begun to turn golden blonde with the sun. The hair on her legs was gone thanks to the Nair. Her boobs grew and her waist narrowed. Her dark Hungarian looks were now becoming a thing to be admired instead of something to be ridiculed.

Nikki didn't look anything like her sister. Her hair was light brown and her skin and body hair was fair. She had freckles on her face and her nose turned up slightly, making her look like a pixie. She too had an ample chest and narrow waist. She was very petite where Lori was leggy.

I still had kinky hair, dark skin and a butt that was way too big for a pre-teen. I started my period but it did nothing for my boobs and waist. My thighs still had the same rolls that my grandmother once thought were adorable so the short shorts worn by Nikki and Lori were still out of the question for me. I was trying hard to lose the weight but it seemed that I would never be free of the "big" girl moniker.

One day a girl in my class who also struggled with her weight told me that her doctor gave her a pill to control her appetite. She started taking them several weeks before and I already noticed the difference in her. By the end of the month she had dropped fifteen pounds.

I wanted this pill. I needed this pill, but since my family didn't have health insurance, a trip to the doctor if I wasn't sick was out of the question. I would never ask my mother to spend hard earned cash on such an extravagance, but Debbie's parents were rich. They had health insurance and more. Since Debbie was an only child she got anything she wanted. Even a horse.

When Debbie told me that she stopped taking her pills because she hated the way they made her feel, I convinced her to let me buy them from her with my babysitting money. It was then that my love affair with Black Beauties began. Those little black pills were miracle workers. I was hardly hungry at all. Most days I skipped breakfast, lunch and only ate a salad for dinner. The weight just melted away.

My new problem was clothing. Since I spent all my babysitting money on the pills I didn't have anything left to buy clothes that fit. I couldn't ask my mother for the money. She had just purchased new clothes for me when I started school. So I did the only thing I could think of. Armed with my grandmother's sewing machine and the few facts about sewing that I learned in Home Economics, I began altering the clothes myself.

By the time summer rolled around my size thirty-six Levi's were cut down to a size twenty-six. Rather badly I might add. I didn't even have the good sense to remove the back pockets before taking the pants in. I looked ridiculous.

My mom was so proud of me for losing the weight that she bought me new jeans in my new size with tops to match. No one, except Grandma Albert, questioned this amazing transformation or the fact that I was so wired that I cleaned the house every day without being asked, and mowed the lawn once a week.

"Che fa?" (What do you do?) Grandma asked me as I was raking leaves from the lawn. My grandmother only spoke Italian. It was her way of protesting the fact that my grandfather forced her to come to America.

"Nothing, Grandma," I replied in English, a language she thoroughly understood even though she refused to speak it. "I'm just helping out."

Grandma Albert was suspicious. "Vene qua. Mangia." (come here and eat).

"I'm not hungry," I said as I went around to the other side of the house to escape her.

It was true. I had no desire to eat and sleep was totally out of the question. But it didn't matter. I would just pop a pill at the beginning of the day and I was good to go. As far as everyone else in the family was concerned, I finally grew into my body and lost my baby fat—all one hundred pounds of it.

Life was good for me during that period of time. I grew my hair long and learned to use products so it would curl down my back. I wore skimpy shirts and tight jeans (shorts were still out of the question because my legs were still chunky). Instead I wore skirts. They were great for hiding flaws. I even started a new trend in school. Girls who once came to school in sloppy jeans and "t" shirts were now "dressing up" because Lori, Nikki and I had finally become the "in crowd".

By day we would strut our stuff in school. By night we strutted our stuff in the park outside the pool. Kids who hated us the year before were now begging us to accept them into our group. Every guy wanted to date us. Every girl envied us. We were the talk of our little town.

Then one day my world fell apart. Debbie announced she was moving. My supply of diet pills was about to dry up and I would have to rely on will power to keep my weight under control.

I stretched my stash out as long as I possibly could, only taking the pills on weekends and every other day so they would last longer. When I finally ran out, I used my extra cash to buy cigarettes to keep me from eating. I chewed gum and ate lots of lettuce, but the battle wasn't one I was prepared for and soon I began falling into my old eating habits. I went back to over the counter diet pills—three at a time, twice a day, but nothing worked like those little black pills.

I could feel my clothes getting tighter on me. I didn't know what to do.

That winter I caught the flu and a whole new world opened up to me. I spent three days in the bathroom vomiting up anything I ate. When I emerged from my sick bed I was five pounds lighter. This put a thought in my head. If vomiting made me lose weight then I could get rid of whatever I ate and never get fat.

So I was back to binge eating whenever I felt bad about myself and then I would go into the bathroom to purge. Simple.

I continued that practice until the news reported that Karen Carpenter had died of Anorexia and Bulimia. At first I dismissed the information. That wasn't what I was doing! Was it? When I read about what she had done to her body I became terrified.

That day I ate and I didn't stop.

CHAPTER SIX

Love and the Teenage Girl

If you think being a teenager is difficult, raising one is doubly so. A teenager is a completely different creature than the cute little child from which it morphed. In fact, the behavior of the average teenager is so bizarre that it has been known to create doubt as to whether or not it is still a form of human being. For instance, teenagers don't easily tolerate those outside of their own kind. They are mostly nocturnal. They are seemingly deaf and blind judging by the volume of their music and their freakish wardrobe. They also seem to have their wiring crossed because they have trouble understanding simple instructions uttered by an adult but can easily master complicated electronics just by glancing at the object. Indeed, teenagers are dangerous, cunning creatures.

I state these facts with confidence because I was a teenager—a lying, scheming, rebellious one who had all the adults in her life thoroughly snowed.

My parents, bless their hearts, thought I was a perfect angel—a bit outspoken but perfect none-the-less. The reason for their misconception is the standard by which most parents measure their teenagers—their grades in school. I was an honor student throughout my entire school experience. Hence, it only followed that I must have been a good girl. That's how it usually works, right? Good grades equal a good kid. Not exactly.

Just because a teenager gets good grades in school, holds down a part time job and has never been brought home by the police, doesn't mean that it is behaving itself outside the home.

Now don't get me wrong—I didn't set out to be a bad kid. As I stated before, my whole life up until that time, was spent vying for praise and adoration from the adults I came into contact with. It was how I measured my own self-worth. But after losing one hundred pounds people began paying attention to me without me having to do anything to earn it. And when I say people I specifically mean the male of the species. Turns out that under all the flab I was built just like my mother. I had an ample bosom, a narrow waist, and full hips. Not every man's dream, but no nightmare either.

For once in my life, people were admiring my looks and I had no idea what I was supposed to do about it.

Before that when boys (and girls) stared at me it was because I was fat. I didn't have to imagine what they thought about me because they would just say it out loud. Comments like, "Oh my God, she's so fat she can barely move," or, "There isn't a part of her body that doesn't jiggle when she walks," were usually uttered within my earshot. Now boys were paying me compliments and when one did I reacted the only way I knew how-I fell in love with him.

It wasn't just one guy who paid me a compliment—it was a whole slew of them. There was the radio station disc jockey; several members of pop bands; the owner of the limo company; the actor; and then a few dozen run of the mill high school guys. All of them hurling compliments my way and all of them quite surprised when it didn't take much more than that to acquire my complete attention.

My most notable romantic encounter was with the bass player of a rock band. I won't mention his name for many reasons. Let's just say that he is known for his romantic liaisons (as all bass players seem to be).

Anyway, like most groupies I was head over heels for this rock star. Like a thousand other girls my age, I wrote to him and enclosed a picture. I told him that I was a twenty-two-year-old waitress from Florida and that the next time he was in the area he should give me a ring.

Of course there was no response. It was widely known that he was dating a woman who was a superstar in her own right. I went on with my life, secretly hoping that one day we would meet.

Sometime later I heard that his band was coming to south Florida. Being perpetually broke, Lori, Nikki and I did everything we could think of to get free concert tickets. We entered every contest our local radio station held to win the tickets. When we were shut out, we went down to the station begging the disc jockeys to let us do odd jobs in exchange for the tickets. That didn't work either. We tried other radio stations and other contests—all to no avail. We were desperate and the seats were going fast. It took a redoubling of babysitting gigs and increased chores for us to cobble together enough money to finally purchase tickets for the worst seats the Sportatorium had to offer. We didn't care—we were going to see our band.

I only had one more hurdle to get over and that was my parents. You see, they had planned a vacation to New York to visit family and they weren't planning to return until the day after the concert. It took lots of cajoling and a fair bit of lying to convince them to let me fly back home a couple of days early so that I could go to the concert. Grandma and Grandpa were right next door to keep an eye on me, and Lori and Nikki's dad was going to drive us to the Sportatorium and pick us up when the concert was over. There was no reason they shouldn't trust me to be safe (poor folks never saw it coming-TEENAGER). Eventually they agreed. Life couldn't get much better than that—until it happened.

The night before the concert I decided to phone the hotel where the band was staying (a bit of information we picked up from our disc jockey friends). I asked to be connected to "his" room (he always checked in under his own name—more info from the disc jockey). To my delight "he" picked up the phone.

It took me a couple of minutes to believe it was true—but I knew it was him. I knew his voice—I knew everything about him. The man I idolized was on the other end of the phone inviting me to come to his room so I could meet him.

Okay, okay—we all know where this is going. Even at that age I knew that he only wanted to meet me so he could add another notch to his belt, but somewhere in that fantasy world of a teenager I imagined that once he met me he would fall head over heels for me and take me away to live happily ever after. Why not? I had read that he broke up with his mega rock star girlfriend. I could have been "the one." (Key thing to remember here—I was a teenager therefore none of this can be held against me.)

That fantasy played out in my head the whole drive there (in the car I 'borrowed' from my parents which I rolled out of the driveway before I started it so my grandparents wouldn't notice I was gone). It was odd that my nerves didn't kick in until I was standing outside his door about to knock. In that split second, panic set in.

I remember thinking that once he got a good look at me he was going to burst out laughing then slam the door in my face. After all how could I, the fat kid from New York, be in the same league as the mega stars, playboy bunnies and hundreds of other beautiful women this man had dated? The obvious answer was that I couldn't. I was just about to walk away when the door swung open and there he stood.

I remember staring at him for what seemed an eternity. He didn't laugh at me, but he did smile. Then he invited me in. He wasn't a particularly handsome guy, but he was charming. What impressed me most about him was that he had intimately known so many beautiful women yet he actually seemed to enjoy spending time with me. I couldn't seem to get my head around it and it must have showed because he kept asking me why I was so nervous.

Me? Nervous? A formerly obese teenager in a hotel room with a mega rock star while my parents were a thousand miles away and my best friends were in my house ready to answer the phone in case they called. Now what did I have to be nervous about?

I won't bore you with the details but I will say that we spent a surprisingly lovely evening together. We had dinner and talked about his music. We reminisced about New York City during the time when his band was just starting out. He even played me a new song he was working on and asked for my opinion. I managed to get through the evening without blurting out the truth about my age or professing my undying love for him (that part amazed me.)

Before I left he gave me back stage passes for the show the next day and told me that he really hoped he could see me again. That was all I needed. I glided home on a cloud and the next day, Lori, Nikki and I began making plans for how we would get to the Sportatorium in style (we had three backstage passes so we couldn't show up to the place in the back seat of their father's station wagon).

We decided that the only way to do this right was to hire a limousine. We called every number in the phone book to try to find a company that could take us there and back for the forty bucks we had to spend. We finally found one that would take us one way for the money. We booked it. We would worry about getting home later (teenagers).

We told Lori and Nikki's dad that we won the backstage passes in a radio contest and that they were sending a limousine for us. Of course he bought it. We spent the rest of the afternoon getting dressed in the matching polyester pants suits we purchased for a school talent show earlier that year. We were on cloud nine—nothing could go wrong. Then the phone rang.

It was the owner of the limo company calling to tell us that his driver was sick and that he couldn't send the car. Our evening was going to be totally ruined unless I did something and quick. I thought fast. I told Steve (that was his name—you'll hear more about him later) that he had to find someone to drive us. I told him that we were personal friends of the band and of Florida's very famous disc jockey (who, though we had no idea of it then, would end up marrying Nikki). I assured him that if he found us a driver we would have all our famous friends using his limo company. Eventually he agreed to drive us himself. It was a magical night for us and it all happened because we had finally become the "pretty girls."

After that there was nothing the three of us couldn't do. If I was good looking, Lori and Nikki were off the chart knockouts—and because our friends from the radio station saw us arrive to the concert in the limousine with backstage passes around our necks, a whole new world was opened to us. When they asked why we were in a limo, we told them that our parents were rich and had lots of connections back in New York and Detroit (where Lori and Nikki were from). We were twenty something party girls who were just out for a good time. That lie got us a never ending series of invitations to movie premieres, rock concerts and after parties. We immediately moved from the "in-crowd" of teenagers to the "in-crowd" period—and we were still in high school.

Whenever we went to these events, we took "the limo." We were able to do so thanks to Steve. Eventually he stopped charging us because we always got him a ticket for the events we were attending. I don't know if it was because he thought that I was important or if he really just liked me, but eventually Steve and I began dating.

Handsome isn't a word someone would use to describe Steve. He was kind of short and very stocky, but I liked him because he didn't treat me like a kid. (Why would he? He thought I was twenty-two years old.) He had moved down to Florida with his mother after his father died. His father drove a limo in New York. It was a business Steve was familiar with so he started his own company in Florida. He had many cars and was quite successful.

Besides driving limousines, Steve also liked to gamble. You name it, he would bet on it. He took me to football games, soccer games and the racetrack. Everywhere we went people knew him since his company provided transportation for the rich and famous. He had to have the best of everything, which meant that I did too. During those months the world really was my oyster.

One of Steve's passions was backgammon. There was a place in south Florida where we would go regularly. We usually stopped by on our way to other events so he could play for a while. And when I say play, I mean play for money. On several occasions, I witnessed tens of thousands of dollars changing hands. Sometimes Steve would lose, but mostly he won. It was quite impressive, especially for a teenager.

One day the phone rang and it was Steve on the line. "Hey, guess where we are going next week?" he asked.

I could hear the excitement in his voice which caused me to get excited too. With Steve, I never knew what to expect. "I can't guess. Just tell me."

"No, you have to guess," he teased. "Think about what I have been talking about all month."

What had he been talking about? The possibilities were endless. He had talked about Bermuda, California, Paris. Steve was always talking about something and when he did it scared me because I still hadn't told him how old I was. I tried to remember the things we had discussed and hoped that wherever he was planning to take me wouldn't force me to tell him the truth about myself. "Water skiing in the Keys?" I asked, hoping I was right. I could tell my parents I was sleeping at Nikki and Lori's house for a couple of days if that's what he was planning.

Steve laughed. "You're kidding, right?"

I was getting nervous. I was twirling the extra-long phone cord I bought with my waitressing tips so tight that I dropped the receiver. I picked it up then stammered, "Paris?"

"Not yet, but maybe soon," Steve replied. He sounded a bit upset and I didn't know if it was because he thought he disappointed me or if it was because he thought I hadn't been paying attention to him. "If all goes well we can do Paris next month."

Okay, now I was really scared. I couldn't think and I was starting to hyperventilate.

"You okay?" he asked, concern thick in his voice.

I pulled myself together. "I'm okay. It's hot in here is all."

"So, do you want another guess or do you want me to tell you?"

I wanted to hang up the phone and crawl under a rock. I knew that whatever he was going to say wasn't going to be something I could do. "Just tell me," I managed to squeak out.

"Vegas! We're going to Vegas."

"Vegas?" I was thinking really hard, trying to remember what he had said about Vegas.

I remembered just as he blurted, "I got into the backgammon tournament. Remember I told you about it?"

I did remember. He was trying to get a seat at a backgammon tournament where the first prize was a million dollars. Oh my God! I could never manage to lie my way out of the house for a whole week.

He continued, "So I got us two first class tickets leaving Thursday night. I didn't book a return trip because who knows where we will wind up if I win."

I could feel the sweat dripping off me even though the air conditioner was on full blast. I couldn't go with him to Vegas. He was rambling on and on about the hotel, the tournament and who knows what else. I broke in, "Steve, I'm sorry, but I can't go."

"What do you mean, you can't go? You have to come with me. You're my lucky charm."

"I have work," I said. It was true too. I was working part time as a waitress with my mother at The Clock Restaurant but I had told Steve that I was working there because my parents wanted me to learn the value of money.

"Quit," was his reply.

"I can't quit. My parents will cut me off if I do." Cut me off—the truth was that if my parents knew who Steve was and what I had really been doing when I was supposed to be at my high school football games and pep rallies, they would have killed me.

"Babe, if I win this tournament I'll buy you your own damned restaurant."

I wanted to say, "What if you don't win," but Steve would have taken that as a jinx so instead I said, "I don't want a restaurant. I just need to keep this job."

I was beside myself. Steve was the type of guy who was accustomed to getting what he wanted. The thought of telling him the truth flittered through my mind but I didn't know how to begin. That was the first time since I became a teenager that I wished I had listened to what my mother taught me about lying. She always said that no good could come of it and she was right.

"Come on, Hon," he pleaded. "You can't send me into the biggest tournament of my life without my lucky charm. It's gonna be top shelf all the way. We'll have fun."

That comment really made me panic. Even if I could go with him, what would I wear? I had gotten through the last few months wearing clothes I borrowed from Nikki and Lori and, believe it or not, a friend of my mother who had a bit of cash. I couldn't go to Vegas with this man and it was clear I couldn't lie any more. The jig was up.

"Steve, I can't . . . ." I started but he cut me off.

"Okay, okay. Don't say it." He sounded really disappointed. My heart was breaking. I really liked Steve. I didn't want him to be angry with me.

"It's not that I don't want to go," I said. "It's just that . . ."

Again he cut me off. "Listen, Baby. I know we haven't known each other that long but you have to know by now that I'm crazy about you."

Those words knocked me for a loop. This guy was crazy about me? How could that be?

He continued to talk and I continued to try to figure out how all this happened. I hardly heard a word until he said, "You're probably right. I know your dad is giving you a hard time and you can't just blow him off and fly out to Vegas with me. Besides, none of the gang will be there so you'll probably be bored out of your head anyway (by gang he meant his friends who usually accompanied us to dog tracks and soccer games. He hadn't met any of my friends or family other than Nikki and Lori for obvious reasons). Tell ya what—I'll make a deal with you. I'll go out there and win the million dollars and when I do you can tell your old man that you don't need his stinking money because you're gonna fly to Las Vegas and marry me."

Okay, hold the phone! Married? I swear I could hear my knees knocking. Married? For God's sake, I was a teenager. I was going to be a lawyer. I had a lot of living to do. Married?

I didn't know what to say so I said the first thing that came to my mind. "You're on!"

Steve did a lot more talking before hanging up the phone but if I heard a word of it, it is buried so deep in my subconscious that I'll never be able to dredge it up. The only thing I can remember is that I came to the conclusion that if he did win, it would be much easier to explain to my parents that I was flying out to Vegas to marry a millionaire than to explain that I was planning to marry some high school guy because I got knocked up.

That night I locked myself in my room and prayed for guidance. After a lot of soul searching I made a teenager's promise (one that doesn't last long) that I would never trick my parents again or lie about my age to anyone. Over the next week I began dating a boy my own age and keeping my curfew. When Steve called to tell me he won the tournament, I told him that I met somebody else then hung up on him. That night I ate a box of Ring Dings then promptly threw them back up.

***Follow-up: Years later the rock star tracked me down at the restaurant I was working at in New York City and offered to send a car if I would come to his apartment. I promptly declined because by that time I was married with two children, but it was nice of him to think of me. Steve, on the other hand, spent his million dollars on drugs and became a pauper. His whereabouts are unknown.

Political breakfast, 2002.

Congressional win, 2008.

CHAPTER SEVEN

From Teenager to Wife and Mother to Tavern Owner

I'm sure that given what you just read you won't be surprised when I tell you that by the time I was twenty-one I was married with two children and owned my own home. That turn of events did more to screw with my head than anything I did prior. Don't get me wrong—I love my husband and my children but anyone who knows me, knows that wasn't what I had planned for my life.

For as long as I can remember I wanted to be the President of the United States. In fact, my kindergarten teacher, Miss Snea, once asked all the boys and girls in our class what they wanted to be when they grew up. It was an exercise that had less than stellar results because when Ms. Snea called on me I stood up and proudly stated, "I want to be the President!"

The rest of the children didn't seem to mind that choice too much, but Miss Snea clearly had a problem with it. "Girls cannot be President of the United States, Leticia" she stated confidently. "Pick another job like teacher or nurse."

I knew I didn't want to be a teacher—and nurse was definitely out of the question because I hated the sight of blood (besides, white would make me look fat), so I said, "I want to be a lawyer." I wasn't sure what a lawyer was but my father always said that I argued like one.

Miss Snea wasn't someone to abide "nonsense" so instead of trying to explain to me why women couldn't be lawyers or the President of the United States, she just hung the sign that said "housewife" around my neck then stuck me in the corner for the rest of the exercise.

Apparently, Miss Snea was a clairvoyant.

My marriage to Bob was a shotgun wedding. Remember that teenage promise I made in the previous chapter? Well it didn't last long. When Bob met me I told him that I was twenty-two (my fantasy age). I didn't actually tell him how old I was until we were forced to fill out the marriage license.

All I can say about my husband is that he is a saint. He is the ying to my yang . . . the calm to my storm. He has stuck by me through every hair-brained scheme I ever had. Even some that worked. Most importantly, he has seen me through many shapes and sizes and all the while he professed that I was beautiful. If he could feel that way about me then why couldn't I feel that way about myself?

When he first met me I was a hot young chick but then the expansion began. I was a size ten when I became pregnant with my daughter. I gained sixty pounds with the pregnancy but was only able to lose forty of it.

I wasn't so lucky when I got pregnant with my son. With him, I gained sixty-five pounds. That weight stayed with me for several decades (except for a brief period when I reintroduced myself to diet pills). My son, Robert was born with Cerebral Palsy. Raising a child with a disability is stressful. The constant doctor appointments, school interviews and fights to secure needed services was overwhelming. I sought comfort through food and used Rob's disability as an excuse for that behavior.

Our favorite television show during the early years of our marriage was "Cheers". Bob and I would settle the kids in bed then go downstairs to our still unfurnished living room, sit on the patio lounge chair we used as a couch and watch Norm, Woody and Carla until tears of laughter ran down our faces.

What drew me to the show was the fact that it featured the food service industry and that was something that I was intimately familiar with. From the time I was a teenager I held every position that a restaurant had to offer. I even served as assistant manager for the local Arby's. I liked the business because it was about people and I am a people pleaser. I continued to work in a restaurant until two months before I gave birth to my son. After that I stayed home to raise the kids. I really missed it.

"We should buy a bar," I said to Bob after we watched a particularly entertaining episode of "Cheers."

"A bar? We can't even afford living room furniture. How are we going to buy a bar?"

"We could mortgage the house," I replied. He bought the house with his ex-wife years ago so I really had no sentimental attachment to it.

"Out of the question," he replied, taking his ice cream dish into the kitchen. (Did I mention that Bob was big boned too?) That house was a source of pride for him. He ate bagels and macaroni for a year so he could save for the down payment. "We're not mortgaging the house to buy a bar."

Later that year we signed the papers for the new bar/restaurant we purchased on the South Shore of Staten Island. (Did I tell you he was a saint?)

The bar was actually a pizzeria that we were going to turn into a bar. We spent the first six months making pizza and pasta for the neighborhood. I was the cook and I must have been pretty good at it because we were so busy that I barely had time to eat. Pizzas were flying out of the oven and money was rolling in at a steady clip. We didn't have a liquor license so we closed the place by ten o'clock each night which gave me plenty of time to drive across the island and get a decent nights rest. We opened at eleven in the morning which meant I had plenty of time to take the kids to school.

Now you may wonder why we closed down a perfectly successful pizzeria to replace it with a bar/restaurant. Things were going well. Money was coming in. The family was happy. I did what I set out to do even if it wasn't exactly what I had envisioned. So why risk everything by closing the place down for renovation and take the gamble that a bar at that location would be a success?

I'd like to say that I have a perfectly good explanation for you. One that will make you say, "Ah-ha! She knew what she was doing?" The truth is that I don't have a good explanation and that if I knew then what I know now, I would never have done it.

Both Bob and my parents suggested that we keep running the pizzeria and forget about the bar/restaurant concept, but I didn't agree. I figured that if we were that successful selling pizza and heroes, we would be doubly so if we could create a bar like the one on TV. We even had a few characters in the neighborhood that resembled Norm Peterson and Cliff Clavin. So we closed down the pizzeria for a couple of months while we completed the transformation.

The only thing that I didn't think through completely was that during the renovation all the money was going out but none was coming in. Bob and I had a large mortgage on the house and we needed the income to pay for it. I began lamenting my decision but by then it was too late.

I became more nervous with each passing day. Bob had leveraged his dream of a quiet home and family life so that I could achieve mine-for that I felt guilty. I also felt guilty that after all I had put them through my parents still had enough confidence in me to become partners in our bar. They invested their life savings in the belief that my knowledge of the restaurant business was enough to be able to run a successful business of our own. It was bad enough that I was gambling my life, but now I was gambling theirs, Bob's and my children's lives as well.

Guilt is a strong emotion—one I am all too familiar with. I tried to remain confident through the process. On the surface I was as cool as a cucumber but inside I was tearing myself apart. I was riddled with self-doubt but I tried not to show it for everyone's sake.

I started eating far more than I needed to then lied to myself about the consequences. So what if I ate six slices of pizza for dinner. I was up and down ladders painting walls and installing tile. A meatball hero for lunch? No big deal. I would work it off. Oh, and the kids left so much food on their plates (which I refused to force them to eat). I'll just polish it off for them because it's a sin to waste food—people are starving in China.

There were cookies from school fundraisers, chocolate bars and whatever else was lying around the house during my pit stops home-and believe me they were only pit stops.

I spent most of my time at the restaurant, believing that I needed to oversee every aspect of the renovation to insure that it came in on time and on budget.

The restaurant opened a little behind schedule but we were okay money wise. I was a size fourteen at the time. Not great, but not bad considering what I had been doing to myself.

Things were relatively good at first. We had plenty of customers and they all had wonderful things to say about the place. Many of them sent drinks into the kitchen to toast my success.

One of the first private parties we catered was a dinner to celebrate my brother's college graduation. My father was so proud that day (I think I may have mentioned that he was an intellect). More than anything he wanted his children to go to college so we could make something of our lives. I remember when he raised his glass and toasted, "To my son, Albert—my one success."

I know my father didn't say it to hurt me, but it did nonetheless. I had let him down in so many ways. My dream of becoming a lawyer and the President of the United States was as much his as it was mine but my recklessness put an end to that. This restaurant had to succeed and I was willing to do whatever was necessary to make it happen so that my father could be proud of me too.

CHAPTER EIGHT

Bad Choices

The restaurant business was very exciting. It was like being the guest of honor at a perpetual party. We featured live entertainment on the weekends and many of our friends would stop by for dinner and the show. I would sit with them after the kitchen closed. They were offering their compliments and encouragement. Things I desperately needed to hear. But the hours were way too long and they were leaving me little time to be a wife and mother.

Every morning I woke up to take the kids to school then shopped at the wholesaler for restaurant supplies. After a long day splicing together high voltage electric wires (my husband works for one of the largest power companies in the United States—not an easy job) Bob picked the kids up from school then drove them clear across the island so we could eat dinner together. The trip was only sixteen miles long but in New York City rush hour traffic it usually took thirty minutes.

I chose to open the restaurant in an under developed part of town because it was what we could afford and there wasn't much competition. I had heard that a contractor was planning to construct a large scale housing development just up the road from the place. My business model depended on income from those families in order for us to succeed.

By the time Bob got the kids home at night they were fast asleep. He usually had to carry them up two flights of stairs to their rooms. Most times they slept in their clothes.

We were barely paying the bills when the stock market crashed and I found out the housing development wouldn't be moving forward. That's when I crashed too.

I struggled to keep the restaurant alive, looking for new ways to cut corners so that we could pay the bills. We were a year into the venture and we still weren't able to take salaries. I was falling behind on the house mortgage and no matter how hard I tried, each month I found myself juggling to pay the bills. I slowly began reducing staff. Mom and I were filling the positions ourselves. She never complained but I could see she was stressing about it. My dad came in to cook on weekends so mom and I could take turns working the bar. We were barely keeping things together and it was all my fault. I should have left the place the successful pizzeria it was.

Once again, I was over doing it. I thought that if I could just spend a bit more time at the place I could figure out a way to turn it around. That's when I really began to eat.

After what seemed an eternity on an endless roller coaster of no money, long hours and bills we couldn't pay, Bob threw down the gauntlet.

"Choose," he said as I stumbled into bed at four thirty in the morning. "The restaurant or us."

I couldn't believe my ears. Was my husband giving me an ultimatum? Didn't he realize how hard I was working to make that place a success? Everything I had to give I was giving to the business. I was determined to keep it alive because it had become a part of me. It was who I was. It was my one chance to make up for all my past mistakes. It was my opportunity to be somebody.

"We can't give up now," I told him, digging in my heels. "We haven't even given it a chance. Most places take at least two years to get off the ground."

"Well I can't do this for that much longer," he replied, and I knew he meant it.

I reacted in the only way I knew how—I over reacted. This man was trying to make me choose between my family and my dream. Well I wouldn't have it. "Don't make me choose, Bobby," I said, and I meant it.

He did make me choose, and I chose the restaurant. Bob and I broke up. He kept the kids and I moved in with my parents. I took an early morning job cooking breakfast at a coffee shop so I could pay for little things like toothpaste and clothes. My heart was broken and my pride was obliterated. I ate some more.

It took me years to understand why I chose the restaurant over my family. Even now I'm not positive that I understand it all. I guess it was because I had created that business from the ground up. I was the chief cook and bottle washer. The customers who came there were there because of the food and service I provided. It was my way of shining. My way of proving to the world that I was more than a housewife—more than that sign Ms. Snea hung around my neck.

Every day at 4 AM I went to work at the deli. After that I would shop for restaurant supplies then race against the clock to open my place before the lunch crowd lined up. It was an enormous amount of pressure to put on myself and I was beginning to crack. I was snapping at people, making mistakes with the books. Mom and I were at each other's throats. I barely saw my children and when I did I was half asleep.

Eventually the bar became a mediocre success. I was able to pay the bills as well as the skeleton crew we kept on so we wouldn't die of exhaustion. Mom and dad broke up and mom took an apartment up the road. She had taken up most of the slack in the business because I was holding down that second job. Unfortunately Bob's house went into foreclosure. I helped him sell it at a modest profit just before the bank took it over.

Eventually I got myself a tiny apartment above a pizzeria. After much discussion, Bob and I agreed to try to make another go of our marriage—the condition, I had to leave the restaurant to my mother. I did.

I took a job at a big box home improvement store as a cashier. I hated myself. I was a failure. A failure as a wife. A failure as a mother. A failure as a daughter. A failure as a businesswoman. Just an all-around failure. The only way I knew to deal with failure was to eat. While we were living in the apartment my weight ballooned up to two hundred twenty pounds.

I was embarrassed when I took the kids to school. My clothes were all too tight. I was out of breath and sweating when I walked just a few blocks. My hair was never done. My eyebrows were overgrown. I felt like a slob and looked like one too. Bob never said a word about it but I remember thinking, "How could anyone love me when I didn't love myself?"

I felt myself pulling away from my children. At my daughter's softball games I hid in the concession stand instead of cheering alongside the other parents. I didn't get involved in school activities. I barely left my bedroom. I had no career and my low self esteem was insuring that I wouldn't begin one anytime soon.

My mom was running the restaurant and I was only stopping by to do the books. She was drawing a salary enough to pay her rent but not much more.

Dad kept the house. My grandmother became sick and she moved up from Florida so my father could care for her. I would bring the kids over several times a week to eat dinner with them and I could see that dad was miserable. I am sure he blamed me for the breakup of his marriage. After all, if I had never gotten them involved in the restaurant they would have been happy with their life just the way it was.

That may very well have been one of the worst times of my life. The pain was constant; the arguments between me, Bob and my parents were plentiful and the shame I felt when my children looked at me was total and complete. I did the only thing I knew how to do to try to make myself feel better. I ordered chicken cutlet heroes from the pizzeria downstairs and ate them as in between meal snacks.

***UPDATE: We eventually sold the bar for a profit and my mom moved down to South Carolina with a wonderful man named Carl Johnsen (he was a regular in the bar and our mailman. I told you we had our very own Cliff Clavin). Honestly, Carl is everything I could want in a step-dad. I am grateful for the love and support he gives to me and my children.

CHAPTER NINE

They Call Me the Bull

It took some time but Bob and I finally found another house. Dad came through with a modest loan for the down payment and I felt like a loser for even having to ask for it. He said that he wanted to do it; that it made him feel good to know that he was helping his little girl, but I didn't believe him. It was bad enough that my hair brained idea to open a bar caused him and mom to split up, now I was taking the poor guy's money. The guilt ate at me every day until we were able to pay him back, which we eventually did.

Time passed and my family was finally happy again (notice I said FAMILY). Bob moved from working in manholes to working behind a desk in a management position. This left him more time to participate in family events. Mom moved to South Carolina with Carl. Not only was she happy but we also had a great place to take the kids on vacation. My grandmother passed away and dad spent most of his time helping me care for Robert. They would go out to breakfast every Saturday then off to one of Robert's programs.

As for me . . . . I was a housewife with a part-time job as a cashier. Yes, it seemed that Miss Snea's prediction had firmly taken hold and there wasn't a blessed thing I could do about it—or could I?

One day I was reading the newspaper and it seemed that the only news that was being reported was bad news. Taxes were up. There was racial unrest. Houses were being foreclosed upon at an alarming rate. Something had to be done and for some insane reason I decided that I should be the one to do it.

I phoned the lawyer who had represented us when we purchased the bar/restaurant. He was a brilliant, older man who had his finger on the political pulse of Staten Island. He knew everything that was going on in our town and he always joked that if I ever got bored with the restaurant business I should come work for him so I did.

Al gave me a part time job working as his assistant. He even introduced me to the Borough President. I was so excited about having a real focus in life that I started a new diet. One that centered on drinking diet shakes as replacement meals. I lost ten pounds in the first two weeks. Finally my self-esteem began to creep back up.

I had a real knack for community involvement. I liked being around people who wanted to make our island better. Soon I became a regular at local Community Board meetings. My passion was transportation and I would regularly appear at public hearings to testify on ways to improve our roads and bus system.

My speeches seemed to be a hit with the people who attended these meeting and many times I was quoted in the local paper. Eventually the Borough President appointed me to the Community Board. Within six months I rose from member of the board to Chairwoman for the Transportation Committee. I was the first woman ever to hold the post. The pressure I put on myself to succeed was enormous.

It turns out that Mrs. Snea was a bit short sighted with her prediction. Sure I was a housewife and mother, but it was becoming all too apparent that politics and government was the right field for me. In fact, I continue in it until this day.

Eventually the Borough President recommended me for a position with Mayor Giuliani. Following that I was hired by Governor Pataki to serve as his community liaison. I was well on my way to being someone my father could be proud of and I celebrated every mile stone with food.

Since Bobby wasn't interested in politics, it was Dad who advised me and escorted me wherever I went. Dad was my unwavering cheerleader. He was always by my side, encouraging me in all I did—telling me that I could achieve success if I put my mind to it. He never held my teenage years against me. Instead he told me to draw on the experiences to make me a better person. I was glad that I was finally doing something that made him truly happy.

Politics, science and art had always been topics of discussion around our dinner table. Dad loved to debate, and from the time I learned to talk, he encouraged me to stand my ground whenever I had a point to make. That behavior helped launch my success in government.

Politics afforded us many opportunities to meet new and important people. Dad met them all with me. In fact, that's how he met his new girlfriend. She was the President of the local science museum. Dad was in his glory.

We had a small group of friends who would get together to discuss community issues over dinner. There were ten of us in all and we would usually fill up a table at political events and fundraisers. It was at a fundraiser for his girlfriend's museum where dad died, surrounded by people who loved and admired him.

The memory of his last moments will stay with me for the rest of my life. We were on the dance floor and I decided to head back to my table because dancing was making me sweat. When I turned around to look back I saw dad laying on the floor with his girlfriend kneeling over him. He suffered a brain aneurism. He died nearly instantly. For that I was grateful.

As horrible as that night was, I take comfort that he died happy. We were all together dancing, eating, drinking and talking politics before he died. Best of all, that night he told me how proud he was of me.

Losing my father was the worst thing that ever happened to me. He was more than just my dad he was my best friend. The only reason I was able to move forward with my career was that my husband convinced me that my father would have insisted on it. That he would be looking down from heaven helping me to succeed at anything I did.

I took my husband's advice and pressed on but there was no controlling my eating. By the time I was elected Chairwoman of the Richmond County Republican Committee some years later, I had worked my way up from a size sixteen dress to a size twenty-two.

My father's death gave me an excuse to eat. It didn't matter that I was finally doing the things I had longed to do my whole life. It didn't matter that I had risen within my community; that people knew my name and paid attention to the things I was saying. True, I would probably never become a lawyer or the President of the United States but I had done pretty well for myself considering my rocky teenage years. So why then did I still feel the need to gorge myself with food?

I don't know that I have a sensible answer for that question but I will share with you the lie I told myself (you better sit down because this one is a doozy). I decided that the only reason that I was successful was because of my obesity.

(Yes—you read that right) I convinced myself that being fat is good in politics!

Why else would people (and by people I mean men—the majority demographic within the Republican Party) pay attention to me? I told myself that they only listened to my words because they weren't distracted by my femininity. I wasn't one of those pretty girls who struggled to get them to listen to me—quite the contrary. They listened to me because they weren't distracted by my appearance. I had heard my share of campaign romance stories and even witnessed a few. It was obvious that I was far better off being a "big girl" in politics. It gave me a presence and helped to bolster my reputation as a force to be reckoned with.

Life at that time was very exciting but it was also terrifying. People were counting on me to raise money for campaigns, gather petitions signatures to get them on the ballot and to help them get elected in general. I drew on my life experiences to get me through most of it and looked for guidance in legal texts and manuals for the rest. But the truth is that there is no book, school or class that can teach a person how to be a leader.

I felt my old fears creeping back. What if I wasn't good enough? What if I made a mistake? What if one of my decisions caused a candidate to lose an election?

I was sneak eating again (odd thing is I was only hiding from myself). People weren't making fun of my weight (not to my face anyway). They didn't care what I looked like—they cared about what I could deliver. But I had already told myself that I needed to be physically unattractive to be successful and that was the lie I was going to stick with.

My first real test of leadership after being elected Party Chair was during the New York State Republican Primary for President of the United States (talk about baptism by fire). Our governor had been toying with the idea of running for the seat himself but my Borough President and local officials had already declared their support for George W. Bush. Eventually the governor decided not to make the run and he too supported Mr. Bush. But politics being the fickle thing it is, ten days into my chairmanship the Borough President decided to pull his support of Bush and give it to Senator John McCain instead.

I thought I was going to die. We were all lined up for Bush and the most popular elected official on Staten Island decided to throw his support to John McCain (just in case you didn't get it the first time, this bears repeating—this wasn't a local City Council race, this was a race for President of the United States).

There I was, the newly elected County Chairwoman and I was forced to choose between the governor I worked for and the man who launched my political career. Worst of all my entire team of elected officials was looking to me for guidance.

After weeks of painstaking deliberation we decided to forge ahead for Bush. Our local Congressman, who was also a protégé of the Borough President, would be our lead candidate against the icon. The campaign that ensued was less than delightful. There was mud-slinging on both sides. I was barraged by questions from reporters and the stories they wrote about me weren't always flattering. All political eyes were focused on our small island. The fight was on.

Most people would have lost their appetite around that time but not me (remember my lie—being fat in politics is good). I buried myself deeper in my ice cream, pizza and pasta as I strategized with my campaign team. The pressure was on and I always thought best while I was chewing.

After a long battle, we won our fight, but the win was bitter sweet. I finally achieved the thing I wanted most—I was a pretty big fish (both figuratively and literally) in a decent sized pond, but I felt guilty that we had gone against the man who brought us into the political arena.

Our success caused the New York State Chairman to appoint me Executive Director of Victory 2000, the sub-committee of the State Republican Party that oversaw the Presidential and Senatorial elections. Better still was the fact that our congressman was asked to speak at the Republican National Convention in Philadelphia.

Even though we weren't able to secure enough credentials for everyone, it was decided that our whole committee would be there to hear the Congressman speak. The members of the committee who worked hardest during the campaign would receive floor passes so they could see the speech live. The rest would be housed in a separate room where they would watch it on TV.

Of course everyone wanted credentials for the floor so I did my level best to accommodate them. I spent my day shuffling between the credentials table in the hotel, where I would beg for additional badges, and the convention floor several miles away where I would distribute those badges to the people who worked hardest and gave the most to the campaign. No matter how hard I tried, I just couldn't find enough badges to accommodate every person who deserved to have one. I felt bad having to choose from among my hard working members while less deserving people from other committees were getting onto the convention floor with ease. Frankly, it pissed me off so I made several pit stops for sandwiches, muffins and coffee to help me feel better.

By late afternoon I had everyone squared away. I was dripping sweat so I changed from a black pants suit into my bright red, sized twenty-two skirt suit so that my members could more easily see me on the crowded convention floor. I headed to the lobby to meet them so we could all travel together.

My committee was gathered in a group whispering to each other as I approached them. They all wore their glossy badges around their necks and I took a moment to silently praise myself for pulling off that minor miracle. But then I noticed the look of trepidation on their faces. It was my dearest friend and political advisor, Joe who stepped forward to announce that we were short three badges. My ire peaked.

"You must be kidding me!" I barked as I moved toward him. "What the hell happened? You gave me the count."

Joe is a great guy. He has been my friend and advisor since I first entered politics. He is logical and even tempered. He's the type of guy who doesn't get rattled. People might even describe him as serene. At that moment the serenity was sucked right out of him.

He spoke low so I had to strain to hear him, a ploy he often used to try to get me under control. "The Assemblyman needed badges for his family."

I took a step toward him and he took one back. "Fuck the Assemblyman's family," I barked. "I didn't see them at the shopping center handing out fliers—did you?" I was furious as I pressed my girth against him. "Why did you give up those credentials without asking me?"

Joe had no answer. How could he? I must have looked like some crazed, red blob, shrieking at him as sweat dripped from my temples, soaking my hair until it began to frizz up. He stepped back into the crowd of our committee members who were all wide-eyed with fear. They quickly sucked him into the pack, looking as though they were worried that I would literally bite his head off. The collective look of panic on their faces told me that I had gotten my point across.

I spun on my heels, cursing, fuming and wiping the sweat from my forehead with my palm as I marched through the lobby to start up the stairs toward the credentials room. In the distance I heard one of my young, cocky operatives say, "Joe, you have to learn to take the bull by the horns."

Joe chuckled, "But the bull just went upstairs."

It didn't bother me that they were calling me "the bull"—in fact I kind of liked it. It seemed quite fitting, especially as I marched over to the petite, twenty-something blonde at the table to demand more badges and got them without a fight. It was clear I intimidated her as I later did the security guards posted at the VIP entrance of the convention hall who gave me access into any area I desired without asking to see my badge. I was large; I was intent on a mission. I looked like I belonged there. I wasn't a threat—I was just another fat, leader who was going about her business. I was a powerful presence. I was "the bull".

Women and men respected me for my directness. There were no romantic notions when it came to me and that was good. I couldn't deal with that type of distraction. I saw myself as asexual. I was a woman in a man's world and I was getting things done.

The pressure of politics was tremendous and the hours endless. There was always a campaign and with the campaign came campaign headquarters replete with donuts, cookies, pizza, hero sandwiches and every other low nutrition, calorie packed food item ever created. These were all at my fingertips, willing to jump into my mouth without me even realizing it had happened.

We won an election—we celebrated. We lost an election—we drowned our sorrows in food. We had fundraisers, parties, and backyard barbeques. Dinner meetings, lunch meetings, breakfast trainings. As hard as I worked is as hard as I ate. But it was okay—because in my mind, I was using my size to push my way into situations and areas that would have otherwise been off limits to me.

In time I traded in my size twenty-two red suit for one even larger. But then the weight began to slow me down.

I tried using diet pills again—the over the counter brand, and even though I took them according to direction, this time they caused me to have chest pains. One day I was in a meeting with a particularly important consultant when the pain struck. Instead of calling an ambulance, I called Bob to pick me up because I was too ashamed to go to the hospital. I knew what I was doing to my body and I didn't want a doctor telling me that I was killing myself.

I threw the pills away then began a new program that centered on the removal of carbohydrates from my diet.

I read the book from cover to cover. It talked about how it takes millions of years for a species to evolve and that most human bodies aren't evolved enough to be able to handle processed flour. So, the book said, eat mostly protein mixed with a bit of dairy and vegetables. However, I interpreted this to mean, "just eat meat".

I cut all bread, pasta, cereal and anything that wasn't meat or vegetable out of my diet. The meat and vegetables I consumed in vast quantities. When I experienced stress or elation I indulged in some bread, pasta, or pizza. I would tell myself that it shouldn't make much of a difference since I had cut those things out of my daily diet. I would call it "cheating a little". And, when I cheated a little, I might as well cheat a lot, so instead of having a cup of ice cream, I ate the whole container. Two cookies were never good enough for me-it had to be the whole package. After all, I wouldn't be eating this stuff tomorrow. And if I did eat it tomorrow, I certainly wouldn't eat it on Monday when I started my diet anew. And if I broke the diet Monday night, I would start again next week.

This went on for more than a year. The diet didn't work for me because, as usual, I was lying to myself.

I finally gave up. I told myself there was no reason to diet. The chest pain stopped and I was doing fine. I had a husband who loved me and we were well past the romantic phase of our marriage. I had a good job and my political career. People respected me. So why should I torture myself dieting?

During an annual check-up provided by my office, I found out that my blood pressure was high and so was my sugar. I already knew my legs were giving out. My limp (the remnant of the Leg Perthes Disease) was so prominent that people were regularly asking me if I had hurt myself. When I finally gave in and went to the doctor he gave me the news—the weight was destroying my joints. If I didn't do something about it soon I would need hip replacement surgery.

I don't even know how much I weighed the day I stepped down from being the County Chairwoman but I can tell you that in a picture taken at one of my last events, I was far bigger than my husband and the dress I was wearing was a size twenty-four. The picture depressed me so much that I whipped up a tray of baked ziti and ate half of it myself.

CHAPTER TEN

Weddings—A Great Motivation for Weight Loss

Several months after I stepped down as County Chair, my daughter announced that she was getting married. It was one of the happiest days of my life. It was also the best motivation I could have for losing weight. My hip was deteriorating, my blood pressure was high and my blood sugar was dangerously close to diabetic levels, but that wasn't enough to motivate me. No, the only thing that could motivate me was thinking about how bad I would look in my daughter's wedding pictures if I didn't lose weight and how difficult it would be to find a nice dress in my size.

The decision didn't come easy. It took time and lots of cajoling by my daughter, Jennifer. Going to the weight loss center wasn't even my idea—it was hers. She knew what the doctor told me and she knew I was ignoring him. So one night she announced that she was going to join because she needed to lose ten pounds. "I'll go along for the ride," I said.

I walked into the center knowing that this was going to be a waste of my time. I had tried this particular diet before. My mother-in-law, Dolly and sister-in-law, Debbie had been following it for years. In the past, I borrowed their books, scales and various tools so I could follow the plan without having to go to the meetings. Instead of losing weight, I actually gained a few pounds.

I looked around the room at the people waiting on line. They were all far smaller than I was. I leaned over and whispered into Jennifer's ear, "I know more about dieting than anyone here. This is never going to work for me. Let's leave."

Jenn knew me well enough to know that what I wouldn't do for me, I would definitely do for her. She put on her pouty face, "Oh, come on, Mom. I really need to take off this weight. I need you to help me. They say it's better if you do it with a friend. Be my friend."

One look at her quivering lower lip and she had me. We moved to the scales and she stepped on first. She was a bit depressed. Instead of needing to lose ten pounds, she needed to lose twelve. I comforted her before stepping on the scale myself.

I don't know what I expected to hear when I was done with my weigh in but somehow when the thin, brown haired, thirty something woman behind the desk said, "Two hundred sixty one pounds. You can step down now," I was devastated.

Two sixty-one? I thought to myself. TWO SIXTY-ONE! I silently screamed inside my head. I turned to Jenn, "That can't be right, can it?"

Jenn gave me a sympathetic look, "I was more than I thought, too."

"TWO SIXTY ONE, Jenn," I snarled between clenched teeth. "How can that be?"

She patted me on the shoulder as she ushered me into the next room. I was so stunned that I barely noticed we were moving.

We sat in our seats at the back of the room and all I kept thinking was that there was no way I could lose a hundred and five pounds in a couple of months. This would never work.

I desperately wanted some rocky road ice cream sandwiched between two chocolate chip cookies. Better yet, Oreos dunked in ice, cold milk. Anything—just not to be sitting there among those skinny people who thought they needed to lose weight.

I remember our leader stepping to the front of the room. His name was Ed and he said he lost fifty pounds on "the program." I also remember thinking that "the program" sounded like a code word for torture.

I flashed back to the thousands of dry packets of "replacement meals" I had mixed with water and ice in a blender on one of my diets. These packets were supposed to provide me with all the nutrition I needed for a meal. They were creamy and chocolately—but a meal? Hardly. More like a treat between meals. Guess that's why that diet failed.

Ed was from Brooklyn. "How many people here are new?" Ed asked, raising his hand in the air to evoke a response.

After a mental back and forth trying to decide if this was my first time on this diet, I ultimately decided that my first experience was a half ass attempt so I reluctantly raised my hand along with Jennifer and about a third of the group.

"Okay," Ed said with a smile. "Come to the front later so I can explain the point system and answer any questions."

He continued, "How many people here love food?"

Everyone raised their hands. Everyone except me. I didn't love food. I hated it. Every time I ate anything I felt like I was doing something wrong. I obsessed over the food I put in my mouth. I could almost feel the moment when the calories turned to fat and attached themselves to my thighs.

"Who doesn't love food?" Ed joked. "Everyone does." He continued, "Who here wants to be able to eat anything they want without gaining weight?"

This time everyone in the room raised their hand—including me.

"What if I told you that on this program you can do that? You can eat anything you want and still lose weight."

That statement caused a collective rumble in the room. "This is bullshit," I whispered into Jenn's ear.

"Mom, be quiet," she replied. She was obviously buying into Ed's brain washing but not me. I had been on every pill, shake, bar, candy and diuretic known to man. By that time I had blended, liquefied, mashed, added fiber to, puked up and removed more food from my diet than anyone else on earth. I had even taken a pill that melted my fat until it leaked from my body in an oily slick. It was disgusting.

No, I wasn't buying this propaganda, but for Jennifer's sake, I stayed.

"Who here believes they can be healthy?" Ed continued.

The few hands that went up belonged to people who, in my opinion, were already thin.

"Hmmm," Ed responded, rubbing his chin. "Not many true believers in the room. Okay. Who here has ever been on a diet?"

Again, most of the hands went up. "Well, this isn't a diet," Ed said. "It's a way of life. To be successful you have to change your lifestyle."

For some reason that statement grabbed my attention. It sucked me in. I had been on a million diets and none of them worked. Could it be that all the diets were flawed? Or was I?

I raised my hand. "How do you do that? Change your lifestyle," I asked.

"Well, Lucretia," he said, squinting to read my nametag. "You have to understand what makes you want to eat. Know your triggers and how to avoid them."

"Triggers," I laughed. "My trigger is my grandmother's voice in my head telling me to eat everything on my plate because there are children starving in China."

The people in the room erupted in laughter then they mumbled in affirmation.

Ed laughed too. "I know exactly what you mean. My grandmother would say that the children were starving in Biafra. But really. Did you ever think about that? I mean—how can eating everything on your plate feed starving children? It doesn't make sense."

"It may not make sense," I retorted, "but it's in my head."

"Mine too," mumbled another woman who I couldn't see.

"This program is about getting healthy. It's about knowing when you are satisfied. When your body has had enough to eat."

That seemed to make sense. What didn't make sense was that we could eat anything we wanted and still lose weight. And I wasn't the only one that felt that way. Many of the "new" people had the same questions.

"You know," said another woman. "I watch some of these thin people eat anything and everything. They never gain an ounce. I mean, what's with that? They must have an overactive thyroid or something. I eat a quarter of what they do and I gain weight."

There were mumbles and nods as we all joined her pity party.

"Do you?" Ed asked. "Have you ever watched a thin person eat? Sure, they eat anything they want. The thing is . . . they don't eat all of it, do they?"

I tried to think about all the thin people I knew. I zeroed in on my own children growing up. I remembered all the food left on their plate—food that I finished for them. They stopped eating when they were full. It was the same for the other people I knew who didn't have a weight problem.

Apparently the light bulb went on for many of the people in the group, but not everyone. There were still people there who believed that they were singled out by God to be fat all their lives. I could identify with them because up until that moment I thought it was my destiny also.

Ed went on to name and describe diets. Every one of which I had been on. He talked about deprivation and "cheating" and starting on Monday. He hit on every single lie, secret and mind game I used throughout my life long struggle to be thin.

I was amazed by how well this man seemed to know me, but then I realized that he wasn't only speaking about me. He was speaking about himself and every other person who struggled with weight issues. All of us believed that our weight problems were caused by our bodies betraying us. We didn't metabolize food like skinny people did. None of us would believe for one second that our weight was a direct result of our own behavior. What he was trying to tell us was that the reason we were fat had as much to do with the things we put in our heads as it did with the food we put in our mouths.

He asked another question. "When do you over eat?"

The answers were shouted out, "When I'm happy. When I'm sad. When I'm nervous."

"What foods should you eat on a diet?"

"Steamed vegetables. Salads without dressing. Broiled fish. Roasted chicken with no skin."

"How about pizza?" Ed asked.

"No," the collective group replied.

"No?" Ed asked. "So if you are on a diet and you eat pizza what does that mean."

It was my turn to shout out, "It means you broke your diet and you have to start over on Monday."

"Really?" Ed asked. "So you can't eat pizza on a diet and if you do eat it, you have to wait until Monday to start dieting again even if you broke the diet on Tuesday night?"

"Yes," I replied, understanding where he was going with the question. "Then from Wednesday until Sunday, I eat like a pig because I know I will be starting my diet again on Monday and I am going to have to deprive myself of "good" food."

He smiled. He knew I was getting it and so did I.

"How many people have done what Lucretia just described?"

Every hand went up.

The meeting continued in that manner for the next hour. Ed spoke to us and we spoke to each other about the lies we had been telling ourselves over the years. Lies such as:

Thin people have a quicker metabolism;

Ethnic people have heavier bones so they can't be thin;

Diets must include deprivation;

It takes longer to lose weight than to gain weight;

You can't lose weight if you have to eat in restaurants often;

Crumbs and broken pieces of food have no calories.

We laughed as we spoke each lie out loud. Our minds were finally beginning to grasp the concept that we had all been looking for excuses to stay fat.

Then Ed asked the clincher question for me. "Why do you want to lose weight?"

Most of the people said they wanted to look good, but I knew that there had to be a better reason. Looking good no longer mattered to me. I needed greater motivation than that.

I looked at Jennifer and wondered what her life would be like without me. We lost my father when she was fifteen and it had devastated her.

"My family," I mumbled. Then I said it louder. "I want to be healthy so I can be with my family longer. I want to live."

Apparently, I said the right thing because Ed gave me a gold star to stick on my bookmark. "You have to have a reason to want to stick with the program," Ed said to the group. "Lucretia came up with a great one."

"Leticia," I shouted out. My name is Leticia.

Ed apologized for his mistake then continued, "This isn't a diet. It's a way of life. Do you understand that now, Leticia?"

A way of life. A path to life. A change of life. I did understand it. It all seemed to click into place. I had been fat most of my life and I was fat because I really didn't care about me.

The soul searching began.

Since I can remember, I had been trying to prove myself to somebody. I needed people to love me and I was afraid that they wouldn't love me if I didn't do exactly what they wanted. I truly didn't like confrontation so if I wanted to do something and someone else had doubts about it, I felt I needed to convince that person that he or she wanted it too. That act would make me feel guilty and so I would punish myself. I was trying to be all things to all people but not once did I ever try to take care of me because that would be selfish.

Food was the only thing that made me "happy" but at the same time it made me sad because eating made me fat. And being fat caused me pain. And pain made me want to eat some more.

I didn't want that for my kids so I never forced them to eat if they weren't hungry. Instead I cleaned their plates because it was a sin to waste food.

The thought of me taking care of me and putting myself first without having to fight, convince or cajole someone that I was worthy never occurred to me. What an unusual concept. It was something to think about.

CHAPTER ELEVEN

Love Thy Self

I left the meeting with my bundle of books, sliders and approved snacks. I figured that it was worth my while to see what this program was all about.

As instructed, I calculated points for everything I put in my mouth then recorded it in my journal. The program was very flexible. I was given a points allowance according to my weight (mine was fairly generous) and I was told that I could eat anything I wanted as long as I remained within the points for that day. The choice was mine. Do I use all my points on junk food, or do I spread them out into meals and snacks?

I was tempted to go the junk food route to see if the program really did work, but instead I decided to stick with the way I had been eating all my life. After all, I loved vegetables and salads and broiled fish. I always drank water instead of soda. Really, the foods I ate every day were healthy foods. I knew this because every diet I had ever been on said to eat those things, yet I still gained weight.

I recorded everything I ate that first day (which, by the way, was a Sunday—not the traditional diet starting day) in my journal. To my amazement, the healthy foods I had grown accustomed to eating were indeed low in points, but the quantities in which I consumed them was enough to feed two people. I was over my allotment by almost one hundred percent.

The next day I decided to try something a bit different. I would plan my meals and incorporate things like pasta, bread and rice, which I loved but was always afraid to eat unless I was binging.

Instead of two plates of pasta I ate one cup—the amount recommended on the package. Instead of two English muffins, I ate one. I even added cheese to my diet—something I had always stayed away from because of its fat content. But the program said that I should eat all of these things daily to be healthy, so I did. I even planned to eat dessert. Chocolate ice cream—something I never thought I could eat on a diet.

To my great surprise, I was barely able to eat all the food I had planned for the day even though the menu was within my daily points allowance.

Something had to be wrong. I must have miscalculated somewhere. I ran back to my books and began reading and recalculating but each time I came up with the same numbers. I was confused and a bit anxious. The last thing I wanted to do was to go to my meeting on Sunday and step on the scale to find I had gained weight.

I called my mother in law and asked her if this could be true (did I mention that she was the foremost authority on the program?) She convinced me that I had calculated correctly and told me not to worry. "Just give the program time," she said.

Each day I planned my meals and each day I ate the things I loved. I was satisfied but I was still anxious. I just knew that I was doing something wrong. I had to be. I was happy. I was full. I was eating everything I wanted. This had to be some type of trick conceived of by a very twisted mind and it would be evident at my weigh in on Sunday.

Despite my concerns, I followed the plan and when Sunday rolled around I donned the lightest clothing I could get away with wearing in the middle of January, relieved myself before heading out the door then went to my meeting.

"Two fifty five. Okay, step down," the woman behind the desk said. "Excellent first week."

"Two fifty five?" I asked. "Is that possible? Could I have lost six pounds in the first week?"

"Sure," she replied. "But don't expect that every week. It's usually more like one to two pounds a week. The first week is usually the best if you follow the program."

I began to argue with her, "But I ate ice cream and cookies and BREAD! I haven't eaten bread on a diet in years."

She shook her head while smiling at me. "This isn't a diet, honey. It's a way of life."

I walked into the meeting that day thinking about those words: A WAY OF LIFE. I had altered my way of life that week. I stopped thinking of food as a guilty reward. I stopped thinking of it as a way of making others happy and me sad. I stopped thinking about it as anything other than something my body needed for fuel.

I received another gold star at the meeting, but more importantly, I received further insight into who I was and what I had been doing to myself my whole life.

We talked about our family history. We talked about the work place. We talked about what happens to us when we are stressed or happy. It seemed we were hardly talking about food at all. What we were talking about were our emotions and the things that made us human. Once again I began thinking about who I was and what made me do the things I did. It was fascinating.

CHAPTER TWELVE

Mind Games, Self-Sabotage and Excuses

It took me fifteen months to lose seventy-four pounds. I looked good, but better than that, I felt good thanks to my new lifestyle. The word "diet" had a different meaning in my vocabulary. It was now a word used to describe my daily food intake instead of one related to deprivation. The word "exercise" also had a new meaning for me. Instead of thinking of it as a dirty word, I began associating it with moving my body more. I began walking in the park, playing golf and swimming.

Friends and family urged me on. I only had thirty-one more pounds to lose until I reached my goal. They were proud of me. I was proud of me.

Then something strange happened. I was attending a political event with my former committee members and everyone there was treating me as if I were a stranger. They acted as if they hardly knew me. Men who never cared for me because of my style of leadership were suddenly "close talking" me. They were pulling out chairs for me and opening doors. Some of them didn't even bother to look at my face while they were speaking to me.

If the men were bad, the women were worse. Instead of coming to me for political advice they were asking me about my diet and exercise program or commenting on the suit I was wearing. They didn't care about the things I knew, they only cared about the way I looked.

These were the people who I stood shoulder to shoulder with in the political trenches. I helped them get into conventions. I worked to get them elected and to raise funds for their political campaigns. They once called me the "bull" but now they were treating me like some know nothing "girl" who was supposed to stand around and look pretty while the "men" got the job done. The whole situation was disconcerting to me.

I took a seat in the back of the room instead of up front with the movers and shakers. I only half rose from my chair when the speaker at the podium acknowledged my presence because I didn't want people staring at me. I felt out of place in the one setting that had always made me feel comfortable. That night I decided that politics was no longer the place for me. When I left that room I didn't look back.

I spent the next several months surrounded by my family and those few friends who treated me the same no matter how I looked. I was isolating myself because I suddenly had trouble distinguishing between people who honestly liked me and those who wanted to use me for their own purposes. I was lost and I missed the excitement of my public life.

That summer I convinced my husband to buy me a motorcycle. He rode one and I wanted one too. I hadn't operated a bike since my skinny days as a teenager in Florida but I wanted to ride again because I craved the excitement controlling that machine would bring me.

Some people told me that I was out of my mind-that I was too old to learn to ride again, but after dropping out of politics as abruptly as I did, I felt the need to prove to myself that I wasn't afraid to face a challenge. I still swam against the tide. I hadn't lost my love for positive attention. I just didn't want it to be based on my looks.

It was a beautiful morning the day Bob agreed to follow me on his bike so I could practice riding mine for my upcoming road test. The wind was in my face—I felt great in my new size twelve jeans. I rode the first leg of the journey very well. I looked back at Bob when we stopped at the light and he gave me the thumbs up. It was all coming back to me. Everything was going fine.

When the light changed I eased the bike forward. The school-yard where I was planning to practice was just around the bend. I wasn't even out of first gear when the bike began to shimmy. I panicked. I was struggling to steady the bike when I looked up and noticed a white van coming right toward me. I panicked even more.

The man driving the van looked confused as I began to veer into his lane. I tried to decide whether I should stop the bike and risk being hit by Bob and the cars behind him, or keep going and try to get the bike under control. I kept going—smack into the van.

It was a head on collision that tossed me into the air and over the van. As I sailed past the van's windshield, I could see the fillings in the teeth of the poor man driving when he opened his mouth to scream. I remember thinking that I was going to die in that accident. Oddly, I was at peace with it. I thought about what the newspaper article would say. After all, dying in a motorcycle accident was more exciting than dying quietly at home surrounded by family (even in my seemingly last moments on earth I was worrying about what others would think about me. Crazy!).

Obviously I survived the accident. I landed on my ass in the middle of the street. I was okay but my left leg was bent in an unnatural position.

Bob rushed to my side. He was frantic. He was supposed to be my protector but he was helpless as he watched the accident unfold. He commanded me to stay put until I could be checked for internal injuries. In a matter of minutes I was surrounded by fire trucks, police cars and ambulances. As they loaded me onto the stretcher I tried to assure Bob that I was okay, but there was no consoling him.

I wasn't in any physical pain but I was humiliated and embarrassed that my desire for excitement had caused so much chaos.

My daughter was on vacation at the time. She raced back to be by my side. My mother hopped the next plane up from South Carolina.

It turned out that I broke my leg in fourteen places. My recovery spanned several years. I under went three surgeries—two for the leg as well as the hip replacement I was trying to avoid. But my physical recovery wasn't nearly as difficult for me as my mental recovery was.

My husband was having a hard time dealing with the fact that he almost lost me so he seemed angry all the time. I felt guilty for the anguish I put him through.

My mother spent several months with us, waiting on me hand and foot. I felt guilty that she had to be away from her home and that she was working so hard to care for me.

My daughter and her husband came to dinner nearly every night. I felt guilty that she had to work her life around me instead of concentrating on her own life.

My son did his best to try to help me. He said that he wanted to do for me what I had always done for him. I felt guilty that my self indulgence nearly killed me because if I had died, someone else would have to care for him.

My boss and my colleagues at work all pitched in, donating their vacation time so that I could recover and still keep my job. I did my best to work from home but I felt guilty that they had to change their routine because of me.

I was consumed by guilt. I was bad. I shouldn't have been enjoying myself, trying something new in my life. I had a family and responsibilities. People depended on me. What was I thinking?

I began falling back into my old habits. Emotional eating. Eating too much. Eating too little. Ordering fast food. There was no reason for me to be healthy anymore because when I was healthy and thin it made me want to try new things and that nearly destroyed me.

When I finally went back to work at a steady clip, I was wearing a size sixteen. I had gained nearly thirty pounds. I told people that I gained the weight back because of my lack of exercise. It was easier for me to lie than to face the truth.

I did have moments of clarity. Times when I knew I needed to stop punishing myself. I went to a few meetings. Tried to get back in the groove, but then I would start feeling insecure again and ultimately I stopped going.

About a year later, my daughter announced that she was having a baby. It was a joyous time and I was eager to help her. We spent much of our time eating and shopping. We decorated the nursery and fixed up her house. I was going to be a grandmother so there was no need for me to worry about my weight. I was older now. Way past my prime. I began measuring things in looks again. No need for a grandma to be pretty.

Jenn's pregnancy was a bit of a nail bitter. The baby's umbilical cord had only one vessel so the pregnancy was considered high risk. The doctors ordered all types of tests and even though the results were good, no one could guarantee that the baby wouldn't be born with problems.

I knew how difficult it was to raise a child with a disability. Jenn did too. Our concern that this new baby would be born with problems loomed over us. We ate out of concern.

Thankfully my grandson, Ty, was born perfectly healthy. I was honored that my daughter asked me to be in the delivery room for the birth which was recorded for a cable television show called "A Baby Story." We celebrated Ty's arrival with vast quantities of food.

Soon after, Bob and I decided that it was time to renovate our house. We moved in with Jennifer while the work was being done. It took six months.

Dealing with contractors, living away from home, juggling work and the fact that I had a new grandson, was overwhelming and the only way I knew to relieve the stress was to eat (any of this sounding familiar?)

It wasn't until we moved back into our house that I began accounting for my behavior and my emotions. By that time I was wearing a size sixteen very snuggly.

The next month a colleague at work convinced me to join her on her trip to Italy so I could relax. We were going to discover our family roots. I was thrilled with the thought of visiting the town where my father was born. We flew to Bari then headed down to Tricasi. We drove the Amalfi coast to Sorrento and on to Naples. The country was beautiful and the people all friendly. The food was better than any I had eaten in any other country that I visited. But the remarkable thing was that wherever we went, the people were all trim and fit no matter their age.

This surprised me because many of the Italian people I knew in New York were fairly over-weight.

I wondered how a country that produced such delectable food could be filled with people who were thin.

I began taking notice of the portion sizes in the restaurants. They were adequate but not as abundant as those back in the states. I also noticed that the native Italians weren't finishing everything on their plates. Breakfast was generally a light fare of fruit and cheese taken around 9am. After that they either biked or walked to work. Around 3pm the whole country closed down and didn't reopen until 6pm when a big meal of antipasto, pasta, meat and salad was consumed. I rarely noticed anyone sopping up the remnants of their plate with bread as we did but I did notice that everyone ate dessert which was usually sliced fruit with a bit of cheese. Wine was consumed with this meal and sometimes a bit of chocolate. Neither was consumed in vast quantities.

It was interesting to watch the habits of my native people. I wondered how Italian Americans had gone so far afield. The only fast food I noticed in the country was Focaccia (pizza) stands. Focaccia is an airy square of bread topped with fresh vegetables, a sprinkle of olive oil and a bit of shaved hard cheese. The portion sizes were small and the natives usually ate only one slice as they sat at a table in the public square so they could enjoy the scenery as well as their food. After that, they would bike or walk to their next location.

Italians take their food seriously unlike Americans who grab a burger and fries from McDonalds and eat it while we are driving (I did come across one McDonalds in Rome. It wasn't very crowded).

On the plane ride home I took notice of the fact that I filled the entire seat. My seatbelt was stretched to its limit. I overheard several American passengers complaining about the same thing. Their seats were all too tiny. As I looked these large people over I recalled the lies I had grown up with. Contrary to what my grandmothers told me, Italian people aren't bigger boned. We aren't more prone to gaining weight than people of other ethnic backgrounds. Our weight problems aren't directly related to the fact that our food is so flavorful. I considered the other countries I had visited and realized that many of those natives were also trim.

I sorted through these thoughts and realized something very bizarre. Americans are accustomed to excess which is the reason that so many of us are overweight. It has nothing to do with our ethnic background but has everything to do with the fact that our ancestors usually came to our country to escape poverty and despair. They came to America for a better life and when they did, they feasted on it.

Americans want it all. We want instant food, instant communication and instant gratification. We judge restaurants by portion size as much as by food quality. We super-size everything then pick it up at the drive thru window. We move as little as possible then we spend millions of dollars on weight loss products when we gain a few pounds. We are a country whose government has to tell us the nutritional value of our food and instruct our children about how to exercise because we have grown too lazy to figure these things out on our own.

We are also a country whose clothing sizes are measured far more generously than clothing sizes in other countries because manufacturers don't want us to feel bad about ourselves.

We are a fat country that makes excuses for our bad behavior.

At so many meetings and in weight loss chat rooms people make excuses for being fat. Things like, "If I didn't have children and a husband, I would be able to eat healthy but because they won't eat anything but fast foods and cereal, I have to eat that stuff too. I am a victim."

Or, "Every time I try to diet my husband purposely buys fried chicken then he begs me to have some with him. How am I supposed to lose weight when he won't support me?"

I already admitted to the excuses I used for my over-eating. Now I was adding a new one, "I broke my leg and couldn't exercise so the weight kept piling on."

Lies-every one of them.

If I was willing to lie to myself about what was really going on in my head what else was I willing to lie about?

I have always professed my distaste for liars. I could handle anything a person had to tell me (even my teenage children) so long as it was the truth. Ironic that I turned out to be the biggest liar of all.

Some people might believe that lying to oneself is a victimless crime since the only one who is hurt is the liar. I believe it's a tragic form of self-abuse. It robs the liar of his or her dignity. Even worse, it robs that person of time. Time spent covering up that lie and time spent being unhappy.

I came to the realization that I didn't love myself. I always stopped short of succeeding because I didn't think I was worth it. And on those occasions when I was on the road to success I either quit before I achieved it or sabotaged myself so it was unachievable.

I was a liar and I vowed that day to never lie to myself, or anyone else, again.

CHAPTER THIRTEEN

Starting All Over Again

I spent a fair amount of time considering all that had transpired in my life. By some people's measure, I was successful but success is subjective and everyone has his or her way of measuring it.

For instance, Oprah Winfrey is the richest woman in America yet she admittedly continues to struggle with her weight. For those of us watching her from afar, she seems to have everything a person could want. Why then does she still struggle with her weight? Is it her rich lifestyle? I hardly think so. Most people in front of the camera in the entertainment industry struggle to stay fit. It's practically a requirement.

How about Kirstie Alley? Once she was a mega star on that very same television show that prompted me to purchase my own bar. Though her name is still a household word, now it's usually associated with her obesity rather than her comedic ability. Many people wonder why she doesn't buy herself some liposuction and be done with it.

I can't profess to know what is going on in the head of either of these women, but I did think about them as I once again began my journey towards my own health.

So it came to pass that I returned to my program. This time I was committed to my mental health as well as my physical well-being. Again, it was Jennifer who accompanied me. She was trying to lose the weight she had gained while she was pregnant.

"Two thirty four," the woman behind the counter said. "You can step down now."

This time I wasn't shocked by the number. Instead I was disappointed by the fact that after all that time on program, I hadn't learned a thing. I gained back forty-seven pounds of the weight I worked so hard to lose.

Starting over is never easy. Actually it's a bit embarrassing. Instinctively I began explaining myself to everyone at the meeting.

"Yes, I was on program before but I broke my leg and was laid up for the better part of a year so I put the weight back on."

I got quite a few sympathetic nods from the group who felt bad that I had such problems but then I realized I was making excuses again. I didn't gain the weight back because of my injury. I gained it back because I never addressed the demons in my head.

"But I'm not going to use my broken leg as an excuse," I quickly added. "The truth is that I gained weight because I wasn't following the program. I'm here today because I need help getting back on track."

Ed issued me a gold star. Then when he asked why I wanted to lose weight-I told the absolute truth. "I want to lose weight for ME. I want to do exciting things with my life and when I'm old and gray, I still want to be in good enough shape to dance at my grandson's wedding."

My brush with death and all the things that came after opened my eyes and my mind. I have so much more I want to accomplish and I am going to do it without feeling guilty.

I no longer worry about what people think of me. The important thing is what I think of myself. Every morning I wake up knowing that I am worth something. I have relinquished any guilt I once had about taking the time to care for myself.

Keeping honest is a constant battle. People don't always appreciate honesty, in fact, some are repelled by it. Being honest has earned me the reputation of being brash and inflexible. I'm not often the favorite person in a crowd of people (or in my family) because I tend to be very blunt. It's okay. I accept it. Now I prefer to be liked by a few and tolerated by many instead of always worrying about what others will think about me. It has changed my life for the better and kept my life mostly free from drama.

Now I try to address any problems with my marriage in a calm and mature manner. I tell my husband what I need from him and he tells me what he needs from me. We don't play guessing games, we just say what's on our minds and trust that the love we have for one another will help our relationship survive.

I do the same with my children, friends and my mother. I no longer feel guilty when there's something I cannot do. I just tell them straight out and encourage them to tell me the truth also. I can take it.

My life is my own and oddly enough, now that I am taking care of myself, I have more time to take care of the people I love.

Exercise is no longer a chore for me. In fact, it's something I look forward to. So is house cleaning, errands and walking to the bus. I realize that all these things are necessary for me to live a healthy life and so I relish doing them.

I find myself to be more organized now. My closets are uncluttered because I have thrown out or donated everything that doesn't fit me. I realize that holding on to past baggage was damaging me. I try to limit excess.

I have changed far more than my dress size (which at the writing of this book is a ten)-I have changed my whole outlook on life and my place in the world. I realize now that my obesity was a symptom of a greater problem—my overall insecurity. I have also learned that there is not enough food in the world to soothe an emotional problem. Emotions are not tangible. I cannot eat them away—although they can eat away at me. I have disassociated food from my emotions. Food is fuel—plain and simple. I will no longer use it as a reward or a punishment.

I have also learned patience. Time is going to pass and there is nothing I can do to stop it. Passing even one day being unhealthy is a race to my grave. Believe me, I'm in no hurry.

There are still times when I stumble. I suspect there always will be. Even now I am struggling to lose those last few pounds to achieve my goal weight. But stumbling is human and it doesn't mean that I have to throw away all that I have achieved.

At the urging of a political friend who knew I was struggling to lose those last few pounds, I joined a public weight loss challenge which sponsored by our local college. I attended the press conference and the local newspaper asked if they could follow me on the journey toward my goal.

At first I was uncomfortable with having the most intimate details of my body on display for everyone to read about, but once I began thinking about it, I decided that it made sense for me to do it. My body is a machine and it should be kept in balance. Weight and chemical measurements are necessary to keep it working properly. Going public with the information would help keep me honest.

I lost sixteen pounds thanks to the contest, but more importantly, I gained enough confidence to release this book. My hope is that those reading it will understand that to take control of our lives, we must first control the demons in our head.

By the way, Jenn was part of the slim down challenge with me. She lost twenty-two pounds and received a medal for coming in tenth place. She now wears a size six dress.

CHAPTER FOURTEEN

Tips for Success

Because I lead a busy life (and because I am now well into middle age) I find that the best way for me to get things done is to make a "to do" list. Here is a list of "dos and don'ts" that keep me on track.

Do take time for yourself every day—Set aside a half hour every day to do something that makes you happy. Read a book; take a walk; ride your bike; look at pictures; thumb through clothing catalogues. Whatever it is that you like to do (that doesn't include ordering a pizza and consuming it) you must make time to do it without guilt. This simple action will help you feel better about yourself and it will also help you to feel less stressed if you need to care for others.

Do not spend money on quick weight loss products—Losing weight is a simple science. The food you consume must be fewer in calories than you expend in energy every day. If you understand that then you will also understand that there is no magic pill, bar or shake that can make you lose weight. Consider it in terms of your car. If the gas tank holds fourteen gallons of gas, you cannot get more mileage from your car if you pump in twenty gallons because the other six gallons overflow on the ground and are therefore useless—right? So how can anyone who isn't a moron believe that he/she can eat thousands of calories a day then swallow a pill to erase it all? Answer—you can't! The American diet industry earns billions of dollars every year because people are stupid. Don't be a moron—save your money!

Do eat when you are hungry—We already established that the body burns calories to keep it going so for goodness sake, eat when you're hungry. In order for you to do that, you must understand when your body needs to eat. Let's go back to science, shall we? After spending time sleeping, your body needs food. It informs you of this need by making your stomach grumble (similar to the sound a car makes when it is about to run out of gas). Your body is a machine, treat it like one. Don't skip breakfast and lunch so that you can save yourself for a "big" meal at dinner (remember the gas tank?)

Eat when you wake up then again the next time your stomach grumbles. Eat until you are satisfied, and by satisfied I don't mean that feeling when the waist of your pants begins to dig into your gut. Eat just enough to satisfy your hunger. If you drink a glass of water with your meal, and include some fruits and vegetables, you'll be satisfied more quickly and consume fewer calories. It doesn't matter if you need to eat more than three times a day. Hunger means your body needs energy to continue moving. Feed it!

Do not eat when you are emotional—Laughing, crying and swearing are the way to give voice to emotions. Eating doesn't cure emotions—period!

Do use the stairs instead of the elevator whenever possible—In other words, don't be lazy. Chances are that it will take you just as long to get where you are going whether you use the stairs or the elevator (unless you are heading to the fortieth floor) so why would you deny your body the opportunity to move when it has one? The same goes for parking spaces. Don't waste time and destroy the environment by circling the lot looking for the space closest to the door. Use one that is further away so that you can get in a bit of exercise on your way to your destination. Multi-task!

Do not believe that you are the only one who feels insecure—Everyone feels insecure about something. Even if you are morbidly obese, chances are (unless they are mean teenagers) nobody will be pointing at you and laughing. People have their own problems so don't let the fact that you are over-weight keep you from going to the gym, taking a stroll in the park or even going out to eat in a fancy restaurant. The more you move, the more you lose and the more you spend time doing the things that make you happy, the less likely you'll be to eat.

Do ask for what you want—Think about the most successful people you know then consider their behavior. They usually know what they want and simply ask for it. Odds are that when you ask for what you want there will be someone who is willing to give it to you. Don't be ashamed to ask for a special order in a restaurant or to ask your spouse for something you need him or her to give you. Worse than hearing someone say "no" is the feeling that you are being deprived of something because you didn't have the guts to ask for it.

Do not believe that bigger is better—When it comes to food the word super-size should never be used. Remember the gas tank. We don't need to super-size anything. Believe it or not "small" on a fast food menu is usually the right size for most grown adults. If you like fast food, order a small with a bottle of water and eat it slowly. See how it makes you feel.

Do read the nutritional labels—Even though our government mandates nutritional labels for everything, most American's never read those labels. You might be surprised to learn that some things we consider to be single serving really contains two or more servings. Read the label so you know what you are putting in your tank.

Do not try to avoid a craving—Most people believe they need to deprive themselves of certain foods in order to lose weight. This is absolutely untrue and may well be the reason why most diets fail. If you want a piece of chocolate, have a piece of chocolate. If you want ice cream, eat ice cream. Denying yourself something your palate is craving will only cause you to eat more of something else. Satisfy your craving with one serving (read the label) of the item you crave then congratulate yourself for being sensible.

Do buy new clothes when you lose weight—Losing weight is cause to celebrate so when you get into a smaller size, buy yourself clothes that fit. Holding on to your fat clothes in case you get fat again is stupid because . . . . (I don't really need to tell you why it's stupid, do I?) Saving your fat clothes is a way of sabotaging yourself. Don't do it! If money is the problem, don't worry. Once you stop buying all those foolish weight loss products and begin cutting down on your food bill, you'll have plenty of money to buy new clothes.

Don't get impatient—Weight loss happens in fits and starts. Some weeks you'll lose and some weeks you won't. Sometimes you may even gain a little back. The key is to have patience. Remember that you are not on a diet you are changing your lifestyle. And for goodness sake, don't give up on yourself if you slip back into a bad habit now and again. Our bodies may be machines but our minds certainly aren't. We make mistakes and we can correct them. The important thing is to recognize what you did wrong, correct it and move on.

Do buy a scale and use it—You need a scale to keep you on track. It's a way of measuring your success. The number is the number. You have the power to change it for the better or the worse. Remember that.

Don't lie to yourself—Need I say more?

CHAPTER FIFTEEN

The Single Greatest Weight Loss Tip
Anyone Will Ever Give You

If you're anything like me you'll be standing in the store reading this page while deciding whether or not to purchase this book. That's why I decided to put the single greatest weight loss tip anyone will ever give you on the last pages. I figure that even if you think everything else in the book is a bunch of hooey, you'll want to read it after you easily and immediately begin to lose weight.

So here it is—the single greatest weight loss tip anyone will ever give you . . . . EAT LESS—MOVE MORE.

Now before you slam the book shut—let me tell you that the next few paragraphs will explain how to do that easily even if you failed at every other attempt at weight loss. I promise that if you follow the simple instructions below and don't lie to yourself, you will drop a few pounds.

Now take a minute to ask yourself, "Am I willing to try it?" If the answer is yes, read on. If it's no, put the book back on the shelf and spend your money on some moronic diet pill that promises to give you a stunning figure in less than a week. (Good Luck)

For those of you who answered yes, I want you to go home and weigh yourself. Do it as soon as you get home, not tomorrow or Monday—do it today. It doesn't matter what number appears on that scale because it will be less than that by the end of the week.

Now write that number down along with the items of clothing you were wearing when you weighed yourself (you want to wear the same or similar clothes when you weigh yourself at the end of the week.)

Now I want you to eat whatever you would normally eat for your next meal. Big Mac and fries, Subway sandwiches, Kentucky Fried Chicken, cakes, cookies, ice cream . . . . anything. Whatever you were planning to eat just eat it in the same portion size that you're accustomed to . . . however, when you get down to the last bite, I want you to leave it on your plate (or in the wrapper) and replace it with an eight ounce glass of water instead.

When I say you need to leave your last bite, I mean a "normal" bite. Not crumbs or broken bits. I mean bite (enough to fill your mouth). If it's a burger I want you to leave that last hunk. If it's fries, I want you to leave the three or four you usually shove in your mouth (be honest with yourself because we all do it).

For your next meal or snack, I want you to do the same thing. Leave the last, full bite and replace it with an eight ounce glass of water. Do this for everything you put in your mouth. Never, ever finish that last bite—and for goodness sake, don't finish anyone else's last bite—even your kid's.

Follow this simple rule for everything you eat for the next week and I promise that at the end of the seventh day you will weigh less than when you started.

Leaving that last bite will do as much for your mental well-being as it will for your physical well-being so you must not replace it with anything other than water. The idea is to reduce your food in-take gradually so be certain to try to stick to your normal eating habits. Remember—if you try to replace that last bite with something other than water, you will only be cheating yourself.

If you want to help the process along, you may consider moving a bit more. I'm not suggesting that you run out and join a gym but I am recommending that you do simple things to burn some calories like: park your car further away; take the stairs instead of the elevator; instead of asking your kids or spouse to get things for you, get up from the couch and get it yourself.

If you want to be a bit more adventurous, try working out in your bathroom after your shower (don't laugh—it works). Do a minute each worth of squats, push-ups against your vanity, stand-up abdominal crunches and waist twists. It should only take you five minutes but after a week you will really see results.

These simple movements will help you to break bad habits and form new, healthier ones. Moving is very important to the human body. With today's sedentary lifestyle, more people are dying from "complications due to obesity" than ever before. Translated into simple English that means, "People are dying because they are fat and lazy." The medical world uses flowery speak so we won't feel bad about ourselves—liars! Just imagine what it would look like if our obituaries told the truth:

"She died because she was addicted to ham."

Not exactly what you want your friends and family reading in the newspaper—huh?

So let's do a recap of what we have learned. In order to lose weight you must eat less and move more. You can accomplish this by replacing the last bite of everything you eat with a glass of water and by making a conscious effort not to be lazy. Perfect!

I truly hope that you try this out for just seven days. Then, when you actually lose some weight, you can go back and read the rest of the book.